THE Bride

RENEWING OUR PASSION FOR THE CHURCH

BIBLE STUDY GUIDE

From the Bible-teaching ministry of

CHARLES R. SWINDOLL

INSIGHT FOR LIVING

Chuck graduated in 1963 from Dallas Theological Seminary, where he now serves as the school's fourth president, helping to prepare a new generation of men and women for the ministry. Chuck has served in pastorates in three states: Massachusetts, Texas, and California, including almost twenty-three years at the First Evangelical Free Church in Fullerton, California. His sermon messages have been aired over radio since 1979 as the *Insight for Living* broadcast. A best-selling author, Chuck has written numerous books and booklets on many subjects.

Based on the outlines and transcripts of Chuck's sermons, the study guide text is co-authored by Gary Matlack, a graduate of Texas Tech University and Dallas Theological Seminary. He also wrote the Living Insights sections.

Editor in Chief:
Cynthia Swindoll

Coauthor of Text:
Gary Matlack

Assistant Editor:
Wendy Peterson

Copy Editors:
Tom Kimber
Glenda Schlahta

Editorial Assistant:
Nancy Hubbard

Text Designer:
Gary Lett

Publishing System Specialist:
Bob Haskins

**Director, Communications and
Marketing Division:**
Deedee Snyder

Marketing Manager:
Alene Cooper

Project Coordinator:
Colette Muse

Production Manager:
John Norton

Printer:
Sinclair Printing Company

Unless otherwise identified, all Scripture references are from the New American Standard Bible, © The Lockman Foundation 1960, 1962, 1963, 1968, 1971, 1972, 1973, 1975, 1977. Used by permission.

An effort has been made to locate sources and obtain permission where necessary for the quotations used in this book. In the event of any unintentional omission, a modification will gladly be incorporated in future printings.

ISBN 0-3102-0105-5
COVER DESIGN: Multnomah Graphics
Printed in the United States of America

CONTENTS

---

* These messages were not a part of the original series but are compatible with it.

INTRODUCTION

The groom catches a glimpse of her. She's standing in the door-
way at the back of the church, poised behind the maid of
honor—like the dawn about to spill over the horizon.

As the last attendant reaches the platform, the processional
crescendos into a four-measure fanfare of Wagner's Wedding March.
Sunrise! The radiant bride emerges from the foyer and begins her
walk. The groom's heart races. Every head in the congregation turns
to watch his bride. Step by step, row by row they follow her move-
ment down the aisle. They cry, they laugh, they beam, they rejoice.
The wait was worth it all.

The bride invariably steals the show. She dazzles us. She ignites
the day with hope, dreams, and celebration.

Maybe that's why God chose a bride as the symbol to represent
the church. Christ means for His church to turn heads, to turn the
world upside down, and to radiate hope and purity in a world shot
through with cynicism.

But we've lost sight of who we are—the bride of Christ—and
why we exist. We've forgotten what powerful things we can do as
we stand beside our omnipotent Partner. Apathy and aimlessness
cloud our vision. And our reputation has been tainted by a moral
breakdown among not only our members, but our ministers as well.

It's time for the bride of Christ once again to reflect the character
of her Groom and respond to His leading. Such a change won't be
easy; being all God wants us to be rarely is. But if you want to start
down the aisle of the twenty-first century with a biblical, yet excit-
ingly relevant ministry, this study is tailor-made for you. Let's keep
turning heads until our Groom returns to take us home.

Chuck Swindoll

PUTTING TRUTH INTO ACTION

K nowledge apart from application falls short of God's desire for His children. He wants us to apply what we learn so that we will change and grow. This study guide was prepared with these goals in mind. As you go through the following pages, we hope your desire to discover biblical truth will grow as your understanding of God's Word increases and that you will be encouraged to apply what you've learned.

To assist you in your study, we've included a section called **Living Insights** at the end of each lesson. These exercises will challenge you to study further and to think of specific ways to put your discoveries into action.

There are many ways to use this guide—in personal devotions, group studies, discussions with friends and family, and Sunday school classes. And, of course, it's an ideal study aid when you're listening to its corresponding *Insight for Living* radio series.

To benefit most from this study guide, we would encourage you to consider it a spiritual journal. That's why we've included space in the **Living Insights** for recording your thoughts and discoveries. We hope you'll return to those sections often for review and encouragement as you continue to grow in your walk with Christ.

Gary Matlack

Gary Matlack
Coauthor of Text
Author of Living Insights

Chapter 1

OUR PURPOSE

Selected Scriptures

Why does the church, the bride of Christ, exist? Now there's a question! Like all *why* questions, which are so often probing and uncomfortable, it can yield life-changing answers. Because asking *why* gets to the heart of an issue and helps forge our values, purpose, and direction.

So why does the church exist—what is its primary purpose? Why do we buy land, rent or construct buildings, sing hymns, and preach sermons? You can probably list a host of reasons without even thinking about it:

- to present the gospel to the lost
- to bring hope to the hurting
- to provide a place for worship and instruction
- to equip the saints for the work of the ministry
- to support wholesome values
- to prepare children for life
- to provide for the needy
- to stimulate action on crucial issues
- to give people an opportunity to serve
- to teach the Scriptures
- to be a model of righteousness

Would you believe it's not any of these? Though each of these goals is valuable and necessary, not one captures the central reason for the church's existence.

1

The Primary Issue

In 1 Corinthians 10:31, the apostle Paul lets us in on the answer.

> Whether, then, you eat or drink or whatever you
> do, do all to the glory of God.

That's it! Our purpose is to glorify the Lord our God. Whether we're eating or drinking, hurting or helping, serving or struggling— God's glory is the goal. Whatever we are—male or female, black or white, young or old, CEO or car repairman, Canadian or Cuban— we are to "do all to the glory of God" (see also 1 Cor. 6:19–20; Col. 3:17).

The Corinthian church wasn't the only one assigned to radiate God's glory. Keep wandering through the pages of Scripture to the book of Romans and you'll find similar instructions more generally directed.

> Now may the God who gives perseverance and en-
> couragement grant you to be of the same mind with
> one another according to Christ Jesus; that with one
> accord you may with one voice glorify the God and
> Father of our Lord Jesus Christ. (15:5–6)

The book of Ephesians also shines the spotlight on God's glory:

> In Him also we have obtained an inheritance, hav-
> ing been predestined according to His purpose who
> works all things after the counsel of His will, to the
> end that we who were the first to hope in Christ
> should be to the praise of His glory. (1:10b–12; see
> also vv. 3–6, 13–14)

"Church, glorify God!" You can't miss it. It rings through the Scriptures like wedding bells. But in this day of inflated egos and Madison Avenue religion, we're tempted to muffle God's glory under the fanfare of our own pursuits. "Let's get bigger," some say. "Let's make a huge splash, a good impression. How about a television ministry? We need dynamic preaching, excellent music." Such things can all be part of a wonderful church experience. But if God's glory is not the primary focus, they ring hollow.

Let's get very practical about the glory of God: It must be the underlying motive for all we do. That brings us back to those why questions. "Why are we building a new sanctuary? Is it to glorify

2

God? Why do I teach or sing? Why do I help in the nursery? Why do I accept so many speaking engagements? Why have I budgeted my finances in this way?" If we're driven by anything, let it be a passion for His glory.

Can you imagine fueling every action, every word, every church program with the glory of God? What would happen? Second Thessalonians reveals an interesting side effect.

> To this end also we pray for you always that our God may count you worthy of your calling, and fulfill every desire for goodness and the work of faith with power; in order that the name of our Lord Jesus may be glorified in you, and you in Him, according to the grace of our God and the Lord Jesus Christ. (1:11–12)

Amazing, isn't it? As we glorify God, we are glorified in Him. Glory leads to more glory. That's what Jesus meant when He said,

> Let your light shine before men in such a way that they may see your good works, and glorify your Father who is in heaven. (Matt. 5:16; see also 1 Pet. 2:11–12)

All it takes is one person with a burning desire to glorify God. Then that flame touches off brush fires of glory that blaze across the spiritual landscape.

Do you feel as though you've unearthed this gem of insight for the first time? It may seem like a newfangled formula for successful ministry, but it's as ancient as the Scriptures. You'll even find it in the annals of church history. The *Westminster Shorter Catechism*, devised in 1647, was recited by young Scottish students who were asked by their teachers, "What is the chief end of man?" The memorized response? "Man's chief end is to glorify God, and to enjoy him forever."[1]

An Analysis of the Answer

What exactly does it mean to glorify God, and how do we do it? Perhaps the best way to start is with the root word itself. The term *glory* rises from our religious vocabulary like a stray balloon.

---

1. Philip Schaff, *The Creeds of Christendom*, 4th ed., rev. and enl. (New York, N.Y.: Harper and Brothers, 1919), vol. 3, p. 676.

We sometimes let it go without thinking, without appreciating all that it means. Let's see if we can get a firm grasp on glory by examining its usage in Scripture.

What Does It Mean?

The Bible portrays glory in three different ways. The first focuses on the holy light that emanates from God.

> Then the cloud covered the tent of meeting, and
> the glory of the Lord filled the tabernacle. (Exod.
> 40:34)

When God made an appearance, the Israelites knew it. His searing light flooded the tabernacle like an exploding nova. So magnificent was His presence that to enter it inappropriately meant sudden death.

A second and equally significant usage of glory appears in 1 Corinthians 15:39–41, where Paul portrays it as a unique representation or distinctive appearance evident in God's creation.

> All flesh is not the same flesh, but there is one flesh
> of men, and another flesh of beasts, and another
> flesh of birds, and another of fish. There are also
> heavenly bodies and earthly bodies, but the glory of
> the heavenly is one, and the glory of the earthly is
> another. There is one glory of the sun, and another
> glory of the moon, and another glory of the stars;
> for star differs from star in glory. (1 Cor. 15:39–41)

How intriguing. Glory pulses from the planets just as it flows from earthbound creatures. When pondering the purpose of the church, however, neither the distinctiveness of God's creation nor the brilliance of His holy light best describes God's glory.

John the Baptizer embodied a third kind of glory—the kind the church should demonstrate. Listen to the fiery preacher's response to the self-righteous Pharisees when they questioned his motives.

> He said, "I am a voice of one crying in the wilder-
> ness, 'Make straight the way of the Lord,' as Isaiah
> the prophet said." Now they had been sent from the
> Pharisees. And they asked him, and said to him,
> "Why then are you baptizing, if you are not the

Christ, nor Elijah, nor the Prophet?" John answered them saying, "I baptize in water, but among you stands One whom you do not know. It is He who comes after me, the thong of whose sandal I am not worthy to untie." (John 1:23–27)

John never sought the glory that belonged to the Lord Jesus Christ. In fact, his disciples came to him later, inquiring why Jesus' ministry was flourishing. John replied, "He must increase, but I must decrease" (John 3:30).

Glory, then, as it relates to the church, means to magnify and elevate the Lord God as we diminish and deny ourselves. It means being occupied with and committed to His ways rather than preoccupied with and determined to go my own way. As Isaiah says,

> "My thoughts are not your thoughts,
> Neither are your ways My ways," declares the Lord.
> "For as the heavens are higher than the earth,
> So are My ways higher than your ways,
> And My thoughts than your thoughts." (Isa. 55:8–9)

We cannot seek personal glory and God's glory simultaneously. That applies to John the Baptizer, the corporate church, and individual Christians (see also Rev. 4:11).

How Does It Apply?

"How does God's glory affect *me?*" you might ask. When it trickles down from heaven and seeps into the soil of daily living, what difference does it make? Among other things, it will change how you approach the whens, ins, and ifs of life.

When I'm unsure, I glorify Him by seeking His will and waiting for His guidance—when I change careers, choose a spouse, grapple with unexpected illness, or sweep up broken dreams. God's glory ferments in the cask of seeking and waiting.

In my public and private life, God's glory reigns. In every relationship, pleasant and repellent. In all my work, rewarded and overlooked. In secret preparation and public presentation. Whether my position is prominent or obscure, His glory reigns.

If I succeed or fail, God is glorified. If my spouse stays or walks away. If the cause for which I diligently campaigned fails. If my church grows or shrinks. Whether people understand or not. If I leave the ministry or stay in it, I let His glory shine.

Some Suggestions for Making It Happen

You knew we would get here eventually, didn't you? How does the glory of God become a lifestyle? How do we live life so that we can say at the end of it, as Jesus did, "I glorified Thee on the earth" (John 17:4a)? Here are three practical and realistic suggestions.

First: *By cultivating the habit of including the Lord God in every segment of life.* How can we radiate God's glory if we shut Him out all week, then casually touch base with Him on Sunday? We must meet often and alone with God, consistently opening the shutters, the closets, and every room in our lives to His glory.

Second: *By refusing to expect or accept any of the glory that belongs to God.* Our flesh soaks up glory like a thirsty sponge. It craves strokes, cherishes self-advancement. It gulps down glory from sermons it preaches and churches it builds—all the while claiming to be in it for God. But we don't have to give in to this. By openly admitting our struggle with pride, we take the first step toward overcoming it.

Third: *By maintaining a priority relationship with Him that is more important than any other on earth.* Remember Jesus' words in Matthew 10:37? "He who loves father or mother more than Me is not worthy of Me; and he who loves son or daughter more than Me is not worthy of Me." Jesus wants and deserves first place on our list of intimate relationships—above spouse, children, parents, and dearest friends. Let's keep Him there by regularly asking the question, "Will this bring glory to God or me?" The answer will reveal how much of our heart we've given to our Groom.

 Living Insights STUDY ONE

Have you ever seen a lunar eclipse? The moon passes behind the earth, directly away from the sun, and eases into the earth's shadow. For about two hours, the moon fades from view, cloaked in the earth's darkness, deprived of the sun's light.[2]

Simply put, the earth gets in the way. You see, the moon generates no light of its own; it depends on the sun for illumination. When the earth blocks the sun's rays, the moon darkens—its surface even cools—until it emerges once again to bask in the light.

2. *Encyclopedia Britannica,* 15th ed., see "Eclipse, Occultation, and Transit."

Spiritually speaking, Christians are like the moon. We bask in the Son's light, reflect His glory. But sometimes the earth gets in the way. We start living by the world's standards—seeking glory for ourselves, leaving God out of our decisions, craving pleasure instead of piety. Then we slip into the world's shadow, hiding God's glory from others.

Have you ever been through a spiritual eclipse? Do you see one coming? Are you letting the world keep you from reflecting God's glory? Take a few minutes to think about the activities that make up a typical day in your life. Your profession. Your local church. The causes you support. The time you spend. The people you influence. The decisions you make. The passions you pursue. What do you see?

_____

_____

_____

Who's getting the glory? You or God?

_____

_____

_____

If you have allowed anything to come between you and the Son, make that activity a matter of prayer. Confess your preoccupation with it to God, and commit it to His glory. Let Him guide you out of the shadows and into the glorious light of His Son.

My Prayer for God's Glory to Shine through Me

_____

_____

_____

_____

_____

_____

_____

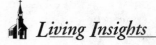

God never changes. What more refreshing truth could we draw from the well of Scripture? His strength never wanes. His knowledge never diminishes. His glory never fades. Oh, the manifestation of His glory will fluctuate, as He chooses when and how to intervene in the affairs of His creatures. And His reflected radiance will vary, according to how His people live. But He is always God. Always glorious. Always worthy of our complete attention and affection.

But sometimes we don't see God's glory, especially when the black paint of adversity coats our spiritual lenses. So we stumble around in the dark, fumbling for the switch that will restore His light.

King David knew what it was like to live in adversity. But he never lost sight of God's glory. Psalm 86 is one of many passages that demonstrate how David maintained perspective. Take a few minutes to read that psalm.

How would you characterize David's circumstances at the time Psalm 86 was written? What things did he do, say, or recall to stay in touch with God's glory?

_____

_____

_____

Based on Psalm 86, how can you respond the next time God's glory fades from view?

_____

_____

Sometimes we need to set aside our dry religious routine and drink deeply of God's glory. No "to do" list. No formulas. Just God. We need to be reminded how good He is. How holy He is. How perfect, capable, powerful, and gracious He is. That He's still in control, still knows our name.

This week, carve out some time simply to savor some of the glorious attributes of our Lord. Drink from one or both of the following passages, or discover your own: Psalm 145, Isaiah 55.

Enjoy.

Chapter 2

OUR OBJECTIVES

Acts 2:41–47

Ministry can be like mercury—elusive, difficult to grasp, volatile.
Pastors grope for meaning amid the exhausting demands of
their office. Congregations gather without a solid sense of purpose
or direction. Needy people flow in and out of the church, some
getting mishandled along the way. Few of us, it seems, can wrap
our fingers around this thing called ministry.

Ten Statements about Ministry

Warren and David Wiersbe, in their book *Making Sense of the
Ministry*, hand us a beaker to contain the mercury of ministry. Their
ten principles and the thoughts behind them will help anyone,
especially pastors and other church leaders, understand the com-
plexities of serving in the church.[1] Let's take a look at them.

1. *The foundation of ministry is character.* "The work that we do,"
the Wiersbes write, "flows out of the life that we live"; which tells
us that our attention needs to go beneath surface activities to the
source from which they spring. Proverbs 4:23 puts it like this:
"Watch over your heart with all diligence, For from it flow the
springs of life." If we want "springs of life" to flow from our ministry
efforts, we must diligently watch over our character.

2. *The nature of ministry is service.* At the heart of the word
ministry, *diakonia* in Greek, is the meaning "service." To minister
is to serve. As Jesus said in Mark 10:45a, "For even the Son of Man
did not come to be served, but to serve." Today's celebrity mentality,
in which we seek great things for ourselves, is more worldlike than
Christlike (see Jer. 45:5). God wants us to serve Him by humbly
serving His people.

3. *The motive for ministry is love.* The Wiersbes write:

> It is Jacob, not Jonah, who is our role model.
> "So Jacob served seven years for Rachel and they
> seemed to him but a few days because of his love

---

1. These ten principles are taken from Warren W. Wiersbe and David Wiersbe, *Making Sense
of the Ministry* (1983; reprint, Grand Rapids, Mich.: Baker Book House, 1989), pp. 31–46.

9

for her" (Genesis 29:20). Love and love alone can transform sacrifice into joy and suffering into glory. Love motivates us to do our best for Christ and for our people. Love helps us build people up and not exploit them for our own selfish purposes. Love enables us to use our gifts and talents as tools to build with, and not as weapons to fight with. It is love that helps us to accept criticism and not fight back, or to receive praise and not get a big head. In short, it is love that glorifies God; for "God is love."

4. *The measure of ministry is sacrifice.* "Ministry that costs nothing, accomplishes nothing," John Henry Jowett piercingly observed.[2] The crowning accomplishment of our salvation cost Christ everything; for He came not only to serve but "to *give* His life a ransom for many" (Mark 10:45b, emphasis added). Our call, like our Master's, is also one of service and sacrifice (see Rom. 12:1; Heb. 13:15–16).

5. *The authority of ministry is submission.* Nothing can destroy our work of ministering more quickly and decisively than pride. So before we exercise authority, we must learn how to submit to it. We must have hearts formed in faithfulness, fashioned in humility. Only then, when we have the maturity to use our privileges to help others rather than just serve ourselves, will we have any right to assume authority.

6. *The purpose of ministry is the glory of God.* Glorifying God, as we learned in the previous chapter, is our reason for being. Not glorifying ourselves as pillars of wisdom and righteousness, but glorifying God. Isaiah records, "I am the Lord, that is My name; I will not give My glory to another" (Isa. 42:8).

7. *The tools of ministry are the Word of God and prayer.* The apostles modeled these priorities in Acts 6:4: "But we will devote ourselves to prayer, and to the ministry of the word." As the Wiersbes write, "if we have all Word and no prayer, we will have light without heat. If we have all prayer and no Word, we will have heat without light. . . . The balanced ministry of God's Word and prayer . . . produce[s] the lasting fruit that will glorify God."

8. *The privilege of ministry is growth.* "If the parable of the pounds teaches anything," the Wiersbes say of Luke 19:11–27, "it is that

---

2. As quoted by Wiersbe and Wiersbe in *Making Sense of the Ministry*, p. 36.

faithfulness to use our opportunities always increases our abilities to do more."

When we serve God faithfully, He expands our hearts and skills so that we can grow in ways we never even imagined possible—our spiritual life can be deeper; our relationships, closer; and the realm of our ministry, larger than we ever dreamed (see Eph. 3:20–21).

9. *The power of ministry is the Holy Spirit.* A. W. Tozer warned that "if the Lord removed the Holy Spirit from this world, much of what we are doing in the church would go right on, *and nobody would know the difference.*"[3] Whose ministry is it anyway? Can *our* spirits bring salvation? Are *our* spirits able to guide all generations across time into the pure truth? No, as the prophet Zechariah recorded: "'Not by might nor by power, but by My Spirit,' says the Lord of hosts" (Zech. 4:6).

10. *The model for ministry is Jesus Christ.* Rather than idealizing and imitating a flawed and limited fellow human being, we should pattern our lives after the author and perfecter of our faith, Jesus Christ. The Wiersbes state:

> If the foundation for ministry is character, where could you find a greater character than that of Jesus Christ? . . . The nature of ministry is service, and Jesus Christ came as a servant. . . . The motive for ministry is love, and God's love seen in Jesus Christ is beyond our comprehension. . . . Love always gives, and the measure of ministry is sacrifice.
>
> The authority of ministry is submission, and Jesus Christ humbled Himself and became obedient, even to death. The purpose of ministry is God's glory, and this is what directed Him in His earthly walk. . . . Jesus used the tools of the Word of God and prayer, and He depended on the power of the Holy Spirit. He even experienced "growth" through His sufferings as He prepared Himself to be our sympathetic High Priest (Hebrews 5:8). . . .
>
> We are serving a wonderful Master, and He has called us to a wonderful life of service for His glory.

The Wiersbes' list boils ministry down to the basics, reminding us that serving in the church need not be confusing. We just need

3. As quoted by Wiersbe and Wiersbe in *Making Sense of the Ministry*, p. 44.

to be focused on the right things.

What about you? Are you trying to figure out why you signed on with the church? Has Sunday morning lost its luster, become a religious regimen? Are you a church leader in pursuit of meaning? Perhaps it eludes you like a one hundred dollar bill dancing in the breeze down the middle of Main Street. You're running as fast as you can, but you can't catch it. Too much wind. Too much traffic. And no one to help.

As always, the Word of God is the place to go for a fresh perspective. In a passage we could entitle "Making Sense of the Church," Luke, the author, describes the very first congregation. Like Warren and David Wiersbe's ten ministry principles, Luke's words help us get a handle on the church.

Four Major Objectives for the Church

The book is Acts, chapter 2. The setting is Jerusalem. The event is the birth of the church of Jesus Christ. The Holy Spirit descends, and the gospel blows through the city with the freshness of an ocean breeze. Simon Peter preaches the sermon of his life, which God uses like a fisherman's net to pull three thousand souls into His kingdom. Verses 41–47 tell us what happens next:

> So then, those who had received his word were baptized; and there were added that day about three thousand souls. And they were continually devoting themselves to the apostles' teaching and to fellowship, to the breaking of bread and to prayer.
>
> And everyone kept feeling a sense of awe; and many wonders and signs were taking place through the apostles. And all those who had believed were together, and had all things in common; and they began selling their property and possessions, and were sharing them with all, as anyone might have need. And day by day continuing with one mind in the temple, and breaking bread from house to house, they were taking their meals together with gladness and sincerity of heart, praising God, and having favor with all the people. And the Lord was adding to their number day by day those who were being saved.

Imagine that! A thriving community of new believers with no

pastor, no bylaws, no high-powered programs, and an incomplete Bible. Yet they still managed to fulfill the primary purpose, glorifying God. How did they do it? Believe it or not, the church had a path to follow, a track to run on that took them straight to the glory of God. And so do we. This passage contains four major objectives for any local church, regardless of size, style, culture, or denomination. Together they comprise the acronym W-I-F-E, which is appropriate for Christ's bride, don't you think?

Worship
Instruction
Fellowship
Expression

Worship and instruction are primarily vertical activities, between us and God. We'll examine both of these in this chapter. Fellowship and expression deal primarily with our horizontal relationships with others, both within and outside the body of Christ. We'll delve into these in chapter 3.

W Is for Worship

Like an irresistible perfume, worship's holy fragrance wafted from this fledgling community.

> And they were continually devoting themselves to the apostles' teaching and to fellowship, to the breaking of bread and to prayer. And everyone kept feeling a sense of awe. (vv. 42–43a)

The Greek term for "continually devoting" suggests a constant, steadfast persistence.[4] The same word appears in Acts 1:14 and 6:4. This was no halfhearted group of pew warmers. When these early saints gathered, their meetings beamed with intense devotion. As they sat under the apostles' teaching, assembled for fellowship and prayer, and took their meals together, the Lord God remained the focus.

And the immediate result of their devotion was a "sense of awe." (2:43a)

The Greek reads, "And came to every soul fear." This was more than music-induced goose bumps or "warm fuzzies" from a sermon.

---

4. See *Theological Dictionary of the New Testament*, ed. Gerhard Kittel and Gerhard Friedrich, translated and abridged by Geoffrey W. Bromiley (1985; reprint, Grand Rapids, Mich.: William B. Eerdmans Publishing Co., 1992), p. 417.

As their worship carried them into the presence of God, these Christians were overcome with the magnificence of His holiness.

Does that mean they sat in rigid formality, too stunned to release emotion? Quite the contrary. Verse 46 tells us "day by day continuing with one mind in the temple, and breaking bread from house to house, they were taking their meals together with gladness and sincerity of heart" (literally, "simplicity of heart"), which erupted in praise to God (v. 47). That's just what worship is: a human response to divine revelation. And when it happens, God is pleased, for He seeks genuine worshipers (John 4:23). The early church, while avoiding chaos, effervesced with the spontaneous expression of heartfelt worship. Unfortunately, many churches today have replaced genuine worship with dry religious meetings. Ask yourself if your church fits this description:

> In many (most?) churches there are programs and activities . . . but so little worship. There are songs and anthems and musicals . . . but so little worship. There are announcements and readings and prayers . . . but so little worship. The meetings are regular, but dull and predictable. The events are held on time, led by well-meaning people, supported by folks who are faithful and dedicated . . . but that tip-toe expectancy and awe-inspiring delight mixed with a mysterious sense of the fear of almighty God are missing.[5]

The bride of Christ, in order to glorify her Groom, must see all she does through the lens of true worship.

I Is for Instruction

A closer look at Acts 2 reveals that the early Christians not only worshiped God, they learned His Word. Once again, observe verse 42: "And they were continually devoting themselves to the apostles' teaching"; and verse 44, "all those who had believed"— which implies a body of truth embraced by the early church.

Interesting that instruction is listed first in the order of activities. Why? Because babies need food. Remember, these are brand-new

---

5. Charles R. Swindoll, *The Bride: Renewing Our Passion for the Church* (Grand Rapids, Mich.: Zondervan Publishing House, 1994), p. 40 (page citation is to the second printing).

believers who have tasted the milk of the gospel. Now they require the meat of the Word for growth.

The apostles considered the ministry of God's Word so important that they delegated other duties in order to ensure unobstructed teaching (see Acts 6:1–6). They refused to allow the pressing demands of the ministry, as important as they were, to keep them from their primary task of feeding the flock.

The ministry of the Word is no less important today. We rejoice that lost sheep come into the fold of the church after embracing the liberating truth of Christ's life, death, and resurrection. But if they hear only the gospel week after week, they become infirm and scrawny. Starving sheep lack spiritual strength for daily living, and they make easy prey for cults.

In case you're not convinced that a steady diet of God's Word is crucial for the church, consider these benefits of consistent biblical teaching and preaching:

- It gives substance to our faith.

- It stabilizes us in times of testing.

- It enables us to handle the Word correctly.

- It equips us to detect and confront error.

- It makes us confident in our walk.

- It calms our fears and cancels our superstitions.

A word of caution here. Instruction, like worship, is only one of four major objectives for the church, one of four supports buttressing the bridge to God's glory. Elevating instruction too high above the other objectives invites imbalance and creates churches with a smug academic atmosphere. Remember what Paul said in 1 Corinthians: "Knowledge makes arrogant, but love edifies" (8:1).

When knowledge remains theoretical, it breeds indifference. When knowledge disregards love and grace, it leads to intolerance. When it becomes an end in itself, it fosters idolatry. Let's remember that all we do, including biblical instruction, looks toward the same goal: the building up of the body to the glory of God.

Is your understanding of the church beginning to solidify? Can you get your fingers around it yet? Or is it still slick as mercury? Stay with us for the next chapter, where we'll get a grip on the final two objectives—fellowship and expression.

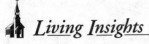

"You shall not take a wife for my son from among the daughters of the Canaanites, among whom I live, but you shall go to my country and to my relatives, and take a wife for my son Isaac" (Gen. 24:3b–4). Abraham's instructions were clear. So his servant set out for the city of Nahor in Mesopotamia, trusting God to provide a wife for his master's son. When God answered the servant's prayer by revealing Rebekah, he bowed low and worshiped the Lord.

Worship isn't always planned and corporate; it's often spontaneous and individual. When Abraham's servant saw that God indeed heard his prayer and intervened in a personal way, his gratitude overflowed into a fountain of praise.

A quick survey of Scripture reveals many incidents of individual worship. Elkanah and Hannah worshiped God when He provided a son, Samuel, in answer to Hannah's prayer (1 Sam. 1:28). The Magi fell down and worshiped Jesus upon finding Him (Matt. 2:7–11). A blind man, to whom Jesus restored sight, responded with belief and worship (John 9:38).

God is worthy of our worship, regardless of the blessings He bestows or withholds. His character alone suffices to draw praise from His people. But what about those special times when God seems so near, so involved, so attentive to the details of life? Do you ever stop to respond in worship?

Take a moment to think about what God has done for you recently. Perhaps He has ministered to you through this lesson or a Scripture passage during a quiet encounter. Maybe the funds you prayed for arrived in the form of an unexpected check. Has a new relationship begun or an old one grown stronger? Reflect on God's incalculable gift of salvation. Or the birth of your child. Or the comfort of your closest friend. How about those snow-dusted mountains you photographed on your vacation? Were they simply part of the scenery or a visual gift from God the Creator?

Let whatever comes to mind serve as kindling for the fires of personal worship. Spend some time expressing your gratitude and praise to God for revealing Himself to you, and write down your words of worship. If God ever seems cold and distant, come back to this page and stoke the fire. He'll be waiting.

My words of worship: _____

_____

_____

_____

_____

You are all called to be Christians, and this is
your profession. Endeavour, therefore, to acquire
knowledge in things which pertain to your profession. Let not your teachers have cause to complain,
that while they spend and are spent, to impart
knowledge to you, you take little pains to learn. It
is a great encouragement to an instructor, to have
such to teach as make a business of learning, bending
their minds to it. This makes teaching a pleasure,
when otherwise it will be a very heavy and burden-
some task.[6]

Jonathan Edwards
(1703–1758)

Have you ever considered the encouragement that teachers of
God's Word receive when their listeners get excited about learning?
Jonathan Edwards has been called the greatest theological mind
America ever produced; he spent as many as thirteen hours a day
in study. But he didn't regard the accumulation of knowledge as an
end in itself. The pastor longed to see the seeds of his preaching
bear godly fruit among his flock and in his own life. Like all teachers
of the Scriptures, he wanted affirmation that his labor was not in vain.

Is God's Word making a difference in your life? Are you getting
a steady diet of the Scriptures, savoring the truth, digesting it,
displaying its benefits? Has a pastor or other teacher contributed to
your growth? If so, jot him or her a note of thanks. Be specific.
Rather than simply complimenting the delivery, describe the
changes occurring in your life.

---

6. Quoted from Jonathan Edwards, *On Knowing Christ* (1958; reprint, Carlisle, Pa.: Banner
of Truth Trust, 1993), pp. 24–25.

If God's Word isn't producing fruit in your life, this may be the time to do some evaluating. Does the church that you attend serve a balanced scriptural meal—meat as well as milk? Is the Bible respected and regarded as authoritative—the very words of God? If not, it may be time to find another church.

Examine your personal learning habits too. Are you delving into the Word regularly on your own? Do you know how? Reading a book on how to study the Bible might help. We recommend Howard and William Hendricks' *Living by the Book* (Chicago, Ill.: Moody Press, 1991).

Are you applying what you learn—allowing the Bible's principles to weave themselves into the fabric of everyday living? Or are you simply accumulating knowledge?

Use this time for introspection, not self-flagellation. Realize that change rarely takes place overnight; growing in Christ is a lifelong endeavor. And keep in mind Proverbs 16:20:

> He who gives attention to the word shall find good,
> And blessed is he who trusts in the Lord.

Chapter 3

A GENUINE CONCERN FOR OTHERS

Acts 2:41–47; 3:1–8

Author Mike Mason, in his searching book *The Mystery of Marriage*, describes marriage as an adventure in selflessness. Though he explores human matrimony, Mason's words also apply to the church, the bride of Christ.

> To put it simply, marriage is a relationship far more engrossing than we want it to be. It always turns out to be more than we bargained for. It is disturbingly intense, disruptively involving, and that is exactly the way it was designed to be. It is supposed to be more, almost, than we can handle. It was meant to be a lifelong encounter that would be much more rigorous and demanding than anything human beings ever could have chosen, dreamed of, desired, or invented on their own. After all, we do not even choose to undergo such far-reaching encounters with our closest and dearest friends. Only marriage urges us into these deep and unknown waters. For that is its very purpose: to get us out beyond our depth, out of the shallows of our own secure egocentricity and into the dangerous and unpredictable depths of a real interpersonal encounter.[1]

For the bride of Christ to be all God created her to be, she must focus on His desires and goals, not her own. We must follow *His* course, row to *His* cadence, fill our sails with *His* wind. The greater the surrender, the more exhilarating the adventure, the richer the relationship. And what better model to follow than our Groom, who gave His life for His bride.

Are we doing things God's way—charting a course for His glory? Have we unfurled the sails of selflessness, allowing His wind to drive

---

1. Mike Mason, *The Mystery of Marriage* (Portland, Oreg.: Multnomah Press, 1985), pp. 34–35.

us? Or do our blistered, selfish hands clutch the oars in desperate determination to take the church where *we* want it to go?

How can we tell?

One way is to take a look at our earthly relationships, both within and outside the body of Christ. Our attitude toward others—whether selfish or selfless—reveals our attitude toward God (see 1 John 4:20–21). A bride who neglects the needs of others will have a hard time giving herself completely to her Groom.

This brings us to the final two objectives for the church: fellowship and expression. Worship and instruction, remember, highlight our relationship with God; they comprise a vertical focus. Fellowship and expression, though, provide the horizontal focus by revealing our relationships with others. Let's take one more glance at all four of these together, crystallizing in our minds a full-length portrait of the bride before taking a close-up look at these last two.

A Brief Glance Backward

In Acts 2, we discovered four activities practiced by the early church that serve as timeless objectives for any congregation. Together they form the acronym W-I-F-E.

Worship: The early church was a worshiping community (v. 42).

Instruction: The early church was a learning congregation (v. 42; see also 4:4; 5:42; 6:4).

Fellowship: The early church was a caring flock (2:44–45).

Expression: The early church was a reaching body (v. 47).

Don't rush past these; stop and let each of them come into clear, sharp focus in your mind. They are the primary activities in which the church should be engaged, the four tributaries that flow into the ocean of God's glory. Follow them, and your local body will be on its way to making an eternal impact.

A Closer Look Inward

As we return to Acts 2:42, let's mingle with this community of believers, seeing how they demonstrate genuine concern for others.

F Is for Fellowship

These early Christians would have a hard time relating to our custom of sitting inconspicuously in church, then slipping out the back door during the closing prayer. They gathered not only to worship and learn, but to be with one another, to care for and share with one another. They came for fellowship—one of the activities to which they continually devoted themselves (v. 42).

The Greek word for *fellowship, koinonia,* signifies a close relationship. Its root, *koinos,* means "common" or "communal."[2] The early church was a close, sharing group. That's the idea of verse 44:

> And all those who had believed were together, and
> had all things in common.

Anne Ortlund, in her fine book *Up with Worship,* groups Christians into two categories—marbles and grapes. Marbles are "single units that don't affect each other except in collision." Grapes, on the other hand, mingle juices; each one is a "part of the fragrance" of the church body.[3]

The early Christians didn't bounce around like loose marbles, ricocheting in all directions. Picture them as a cluster of ripe grapes, squeezed together by persecution, bleeding and mingling into one another.

Fellowship, then, is genuine Christianity freely shared among God's family members. It's sad to think of how many Christians today are missing that kind of closeness. Sermons and songs, while uplifting and necessary, provide only part of a vital church encounter. We need involvement with others too. If we roll in and out of church each week without acquiring a few grape juice stains, we really haven't tasted the sweet wine of fellowship.

The New Testament portrays true fellowship in two primary ways. First, as an act of sharing something tangible to meet a need. Note verse 45.

> And they began selling their property and posses-
> sions, and were sharing them with all, as anyone
> might have need.

What a picture of sacrificial giving. Believers were selling land

---

2. Walter Bauer, *A Greek-English Lexicon of the New Testament and Other Early Christian Literature,* 2d ed. Revised and augmented by F. Wilbur Gingrich and Frederick W. Danker, from Walter Bauer's 5th ed., 1958 (Chicago, Ill.: University of Chicago Press, 1979), pp. 438–39.

3. Anne Ortlund, *Up with Worship,* rev. ed. (Ventura, Calif.: Regal Books, 1982), p. 102.

and personal belongings, then channeling the proceeds to . . . people. Not a bigger or more elaborate home. Not a new car. Not a CD or an IRA. But *people*—needy individuals who depended on their brothers and sisters in Christ for survival. Such unselfishness, as Gene Getz explains, was crucial to the life of the early church.

> When the church was born in Jerusalem, it appears that the majority of those Jews who had come from distant places and who responded to the gospel decided to stay and wait for Christ to return and to restore the earthly kingdom to Israel. . . .
>
> . . . Many had already used up their surplus of money and food. Those who were staying in public inns would need to pay their rent, and everyone needed food daily. To solve this problem, the believers decided to "have everything in common." This included both those who lived in Jerusalem and those who lived in other parts of the Roman Empire. But the residents of Jerusalem had to take the initial steps in solving the problem. This they did—willingly and unselfishly.[4]

Add to these the families who were ostracized or persecuted for their newly found faith, and the needs pile up with overwhelming speed.

Does your church display the generous spirit demonstrated by the early church? Such selflessness seems to be the exception today, especially in the world's financial arena. Surrendering a profit to help someone in need draws more sneers than cheers. Many of us would rather let our funds ferment in the vat of plenty than quench the palates of the needy—unless, of course, we could get a tax break.

Sharing something tangible to meet a need—that's one form of fellowship. The second form it takes is sharing *in* something with someone else. Weeping with those who weep. Rejoicing with those who rejoice. Grieving with those who grieve.[5]

Sometimes the best thing we can give is ourselves. Who can assign a dollar value to the tears we shed for someone else's loss?

---

4. Gene A. Getz, *A Biblical Theology of Material Possessions* (Chicago, Ill.: Moody Press, 1990), p. 43.

5. See Romans 12:15 and its context for the attitude members of the body of Christ are to have toward one another.

Or the time we give to listen to a friend vent his or her frustration? Or our applause upon learning of a peer's promotion?

Koinonia. It happens when God's people come together in the spirit of sharing; when full hands and hearts share with empty ones. Then the body of Christ is strengthened. And, hopefully, the world takes notice.

E *Is for Expression*

"And the Lord was adding to their number day by day those who were being saved" (Acts 2:47b). Is it any wonder that God blessed the Jerusalem church with growth? Christians there offered love and acceptance. They modeled vulnerability, compassion, caring, and giving. They radiated winsomeness and joy. The aroma of these qualities drifted from the church into the nostrils of Jerusalem like a Sunday pot roast. And the world came to dinner.

The early church could no more dam up the flow of the gospel than storm clouds can hold their rain. As believers expressed the reality of Christ to a watching world, the ranks of the converted swelled. The early church was a reaching body. They modeled *expression*—our fourth and final objective for the church.

In the very next chapter of Acts, notice how the church's message begins to spill into the streets of Jerusalem.

> Now Peter and John were going up to the temple at the ninth hour, the hour of prayer. And a certain man who had been lame from his mother's womb was being carried along, whom they used to set down every day at the gate of the temple which is called Beautiful, in order to beg alms of those who were entering the temple. And when he saw Peter and John about to go into the temple, he began asking to receive alms. (3:1–3)

What a predicament for Peter and John. They had no money to spare for a crippled beggar; the ministry wasn't putting any extra coins in their pockets. But they gave the beggar something more lasting than silver and gold.

> And Peter, along with John, fixed his gaze upon him and said, "Look at us!" And he began to give them his attention, expecting to receive something from them. But Peter said, "I do not possess silver and

gold, but what I do have I give to you: In the name of Jesus Christ the Nazarene—walk!" And seizing him by the right hand, he raised him up; and immediately his feet and his ankles were strengthened. And with a leap, he stood upright and began to walk; and he entered the temple with them, walking and leaping and praising God. (vv. 4–8)

Peter and John expressed the reality of the resurrected Christ, first by reaching out to the beggar, then by proclaiming the gospel to the crowd gathering around them (vv. 11–26). Their display of authentic Christianity helped the church grow from three thousand to five thousand in a very short time (4:4).

What reward did Peter and John receive? They were thrown in the slammer, then called on the carpet by the *religious* folks—the same ones who crucified Jesus when He threw a wrench in their mechanical system of spirituality. "This is out of the ordinary," they barked. "We don't have room for this. Who are you anyway?"

Peter, recognizing that God had provided an audience, then preached the gospel to his inquisitors (4:8–12). Threatened and released, he and John took the Word of God right back into the streets. In Acts 5, the apostles are arrested two more times for preaching the gospel, warned, even flogged. But their zeal refused to be dampened. Acts 5:29 sums up their attitude: "We must obey God rather than men." So "every day, in the temple and from house to house, they kept right on teaching and preaching Jesus as the Christ" (v. 42).

Did you notice that evangelism took place *outside* the church? We often adopt methods or philosophies for reaching the lost that the early church rarely practiced. In fact, here are four observations about evangelism in the first century that might surprise you.

1. *Evangelism was never limited to the church gathering.* It occurred there least of all. Believers met corporately to be built up in Christ; then they hit the streets with His message of grace.

2. *Evangelism was always initiated by the Christian.* Early believers didn't wait for people to ask; they initiated the discussion of spiritual things.

3. *Evangelism was usually connected with another unrelated event or experience,* such as intense opposition, a healing or other miracle, a conversation, argument, or catastrophe. Their concern for the lost came to the surface in a variety of circumstances.

4. *Evangelism was never coercive or manipulative.* The lost were treated with dignity and respect. Early believers delivered the gospel with boldness and conviction, but they left the results to God.

How fitting that our acronym W-I-F-E ends with expression. A bride who is awed by worship, deepened by the Word of God, and uplifted by fellowship cannot help inviting others to the wedding.

A Realistic Look Forward

As you look ahead in your own life and ministry, keeping W-I-F-E in mind will help you maintain some balance. Think of the church's ministry in two dimensions—*depth* and *breadth*. The depth of a ministry is determined by its quality of worship and instruction. A church with all fellowship and evangelism may have lots of people and programs, but the lack of the Word and worship will leave it shallow.

The breadth of a church depends on its commitment to fellowship and expression. Worship and instruction at the expense of fellowship and expression may create an elite group of believers who would rather keep to themselves than reach out to others.

 Living Insights STUDY ONE

Mmmmmm. Mom's Texas chili. Choice ground beef sizzled in a deep skillet with chopped onions, dusted with garlic powder. Plump red kidney beans. Hunks of juicy tomatoes. All blended with tangy tomato sauce. A pinch of blazing chili powder (or a fistful, depending on the training of your palate and your proximity to a fire extinguisher). Stirred and sampled (several times) with a wooden spoon. Simmered until the aroma hunts you down like a posse. Ladled into a bowl, still steaming, and topped off with grated cheese or crushed crackers. And to put out the fire? A sweaty tumbler of Mom's iced tea, already sweetened.

Few things can tame an appetite like Mom's Texas chili, especially on a frosty evening. Her secret? Two things: Diversity and time. She combines several ingredients, each with different qualities, then lets them simmer on low heat for a few hours. The meat absorbs the garlic. The sauce mingles with the beans. The onions liven up the tomatoes. And the chili powder influences everything. Before long, you have chili, not just a pot full of individual ingredients.

You might say chili has "all things in common," much like the early church. Every ingredient, like every believer, contributes to the building up of the whole. And time makes the mix richer.

How rich is the mix, the *koinonia*, in your local church? Are you blending with other believers, seasoning their lives and absorbing what they have to give? Is your group a diverse one, or is everyone there the same flavor as you? Do you take time to simmer with others, or do you spend most of your hours alone? Maybe you need to add some spice by entering into someone's life or making a special sacrifice to help a Christian brother or sister in need. You might want to join a small group, if your church has them, or begin meeting with one other person occasionally for mutual encouragement.

Perhaps your spiritual taste buds are accustomed to fine fellowship, and you don't need to change a thing. That's great. But if you do need to make some adjustments, start now. Write down one thing you can do this week to flavor the fellowship bowl in your church. Bon appetit!

_____

_____

_____

_____

 Living Insights STUDY TWO

"When's the last time you shared your faith?" That question can strike a chord of guilt in the most devout Christian. Most of us would love to tell more people about Jesus Christ. But some of us lack confidence. Others fear rejection. Still others think they're not living a good enough life. Many simply don't know how to begin such a conversation.

We don't want to throw a guilt party, but the question is worth considering. As Christians, sharing the gospel is not only part of our job description, it's our privilege.

How comfortable are you with sharing your faith? Does the gospel message trickle from your life naturally, like thawing snow? Or does it reluctantly chip off in icy chunks? Maybe your style falls somewhere in between. Take a moment to assess your own evangelism habits. Evaluate; don't condemn (see Rom. 8:1). And remember, most of us have to work at it.

If you find that lack of preparation prevents you from sharing, spend some time solidifying the gospel message in your mind. Review some key passages, such as Acts 26:16–18, 1 Corinthians 15:1–11, and Ephesians 2:1–10. Make a list of key elements to include in a gospel presentation.

_____

_____

_____

_____

_____

Have you ever written out your personal testimony? Give it a try! Then practice delivering it, along with the gospel message, to an honest but sensitive friend.

_____

_____

_____

_____

_____

Chapter 4

A CONTAGIOUS STYLE
1 Thessalonians 2:1–13

S ki season in the Colorado Rockies. You and your friends have spent the whole day carving up a layer of fresh powder. The slopes are closed for the day, and your cheeks burn from a relentless rush of sun, speed, and cold. After stepping out of your skis and propping them against the rack in front of the cabin, you free your tortured feet from your ski boots ("Have my feet grown in one day?"). Dry socks and a warm fire will melt away all discomfort.

Once inside, everyone heads for a steaming shower and change of clothes. You're all looking forward to a rendezvous in front of the fire, where pepperoni pizza will disappear in record time and stories of the slopes will fill the air like the scent of pine. You pull on your wool socks, button up your faded Levi's, and slip into that argyle sweater you got for Christmas. The aroma of cinnamon drifts into your room—someone's warming apple cider.

You bolt from the bedroom, down the stairs, into the den, and . . . what's this? No fire?

"No dry wood," someone says. "And they can't bring us any until tomorrow."

This can't be! A fireplace with no fire? You stare in shock at the iron grate that should be cradling six or seven logs. But it sits empty and exposed, like the rib cage of a famished beast. Tonight there will be no warm glow to gather around. No flickering shadows. No rhythmic crackling of the flames to accompany the guitar. No gooey marshmallows for s'mores. And hot cider's just another drink without the pip-pop of blazing bark.

"I wonder," you whisper to yourself, looking around the room, "if anyone would miss the furniture?"

A fireplace, no matter how inviting its architecture, is as cold as a tomb if it doesn't surround a crackling fire. All the brick and brass in the world won't make up for the lack of warmth; it's what's on the inside that counts. And that's true of churches too.

Various Types of Churches

Often, we tend to judge churches by the looks of the building or the size of the congregation. A large, modern church, we assume, is full of creative, forward-thinking people. A small, white, wooden church, nestled among sheltering oaks, makes us think of a close, warm, friendly body of believers. Once we walk through the door and sit down, though, we may find that the modern church is stuffily old-fashioned and the church among the oaks has splintered into fractious factions. Judging by externals, as most of us have probably learned from painful experience, can be frustratingly misleading.

Jesus, however, didn't think of His church in terms of buildings or size. When He promised, "I will build My church; and the gates of Hades shall not overpower it" (Matt. 16:18), He was talking about *people*. The Greek term for *church, ekklesia,* means "a gathering" or "assembly."[1] Jesus had people in mind—those who would gather together to worship Him.

So are we recommending the demolition of all church property? Certainly not. We just need to remember that externals rarely reveal what's happening inside. Trying to determine a church's character by its edifice or membership roll is like judging a fireplace by its brick and brass. It's the fire inside that counts.

Four Characteristics of a Contagious Style

So what is it that provides the fire in a local church? What causes people to step in from the cold world, gather close, and warm their souls?

The Holy Spirit, of course, stokes the fire in the body of Christ to ignite lives for God's glory. But humanly speaking, each local church that's aflame for God emits a curious, attractive glow. Call it personality, or better yet, call it a *contagious style.*

The apostle Paul, in 1 Thessalonians 2:1–13, describes such a church. Let's follow along with Paul and discover the four characteristics that made the church at Thessalonica burn with a contagious style.

A Contagious Style Is Biblical in Content

Reflecting on the six to eight weeks he spent with the Thessalonians, Paul writes:

> For you yourselves know, brethren, that our coming to you was not in vain, but after we had already

---

1. Merrill F. Unger, *Unger's Bible Dictionary* (Chicago, Ill.: Moody Press, 1966), p. 204.

suffered and been mistreated in Philippi, as you know, we had the boldness in our God to speak to you the gospel of God amid much opposition. (vv. 1–2)

In Philippi, Paul endured a beating, imprisonment, and an earthquake. He limped out of there, hounded by his accusers, yet resolutely moving ahead. Arriving in Thessalonica, he continued to minister "amid much opposition," but not in vain. Because, despite the difficulties, he still boldly declared "the gospel of God," as he states later several times:

> But just as we have been approved by God to be *entrusted with the gospel,* so we speak, not as pleasing men but God, who examines our hearts. (v. 4, emphasis added)

> Having thus a fond affection for you, we were well-pleased to *impart to you not only the gospel of God* but also our own lives, because you had become very dear to us. (v. 8, emphasis added)

> For you recall, brethren, our labor and hardship, how working night and day so as not to be a burden to any of you, we *proclaimed to you the gospel of God.* (v. 9, emphasis added)

> And for this reason we also constantly thank God that when you *received from us the word of God's message,* you accepted it not as the word of men, but for what it really is, the word of God, which also performs its work in you who believe. (v. 13, emphasis added)

Time after time, as Paul reflects on the Thessalonians, he calls to mind the substance of his message to them—the gospel. His message, in our terms, was *biblical in content.* Had you sat among the worshipers in Thessalonica, you would have heard the clear and consistent declaration of God's Word, not the idle ramblings or opinions of a preacher.

The gospel reaching the Thessalonians was pure, as Paul attests in verse 3: "For our exhortation does not come from error or impurity or by way of deceit." Notice, too, that Paul spoke "not as pleasing men but God, who examines our hearts" (v. 4). God's Word cuts the heart out of hypocrisy; words cannot be deceptive or flattering and biblical at the same time.

John R. W. Stott, in his book *The Preacher's Portrait*, helps show the proper balance between biblical conviction and congregational sensitivity.

> It is not enough for the preacher to know the Word of God; he must know the people to whom he proclaims it. He must not, of course, falsify God's Word in order to make it more appealing. He cannot dilute the strong medicine of Scripture to render it more sweet to the taste. But he may seek to present it to the people in such a way as to commend it to them. . . . The expository preacher is a bridge builder, seeking to span the gulf between the Word of God and the mind of man. He must do his utmost to interpret the Scripture so accurately and plainly, and to apply it so forcefully, that the truth crosses the bridge.[2]

The Bible is our authority. As Stott highlights later, "The less the preacher comes between the Word and its hearers, the better."[3]

A Contagious Style Is Authentic in Nature

In verses 5 and 6, the emphasis shifts from the message to the messenger.

> For we never came with flattering speech, as you know, nor with a pretext for greed—God is witness—nor did we seek glory from men, either from you or from others, even though as apostles of Christ we might have asserted our authority.

What this reveals, in essence, is that Paul was real. He was upfront. No Thessalonian could rightly accuse him of exploiting the church for personal gain. He didn't manipulate with flattery. Nor did he expect royal treatment because of his privileged position as an apostle. No, what the Thessalonians saw, they got. Paul even dared to be transparent about his struggles (v. 2; see also 1 Cor. 2:1–5).

---

2. John R. W. Stott, *The Preacher's Portrait: Some New Testament Word Studies* (Grand Rapids, Mich.: William B. Eerdmans Publishing Co., 1961), p. 28.

3. Stott, *The Preacher's Portrait*, p. 30.

A church with a contagious style is *authentic in nature*. Authenticity is revealed in real people saying real things about real issues with real feelings. No hidden agendas. No pious facade. Masks come off and we live what we are—telling the truth to ourselves and others. Facing our weaknesses and admitting that we don't know it all and don't have it all together.

Imagine a church that models such authenticity. People fed up with fakes will come out of the woodwork to watch real Christians living what they claim to believe.

A Contagious Style Is Gracious in Attitude

A church with a contagious style also demonstrates a *gracious attitude*.

> But we proved to be gentle among you, as a nursing mother tenderly cares for her own children. Having thus a fond affection for you we were well-pleased to impart to you not only the gospel of God but also our own lives, because you had become very dear to us. For you recall, brethren, our labor and hardship, how working night and day so as not to be a burden to any of you, we proclaimed to you the gospel of God. You are witnesses, and so is God, how devoutly and uprightly and blamelessly we behaved toward you believers; just as you know how we were exhorting and encouraging and imploring each one of you as a father would his own children. (vv. 7–11)

Interesting, isn't it? This passage opens with the tenderness of a mother (v. 7) and closes with the leadership of a father (v. 11). Such imagery reinforces the fact that the church is a family, not a corporation with CEOs and stockholders.

Notice how Paul treated the Thessalonians in the midst of ministry. He didn't bark commands like a drill sergeant: he tenderly cared for them like a mother with her nursing infant. He was gentle, tolerant, patient. He not only gave them the gospel, he gave them himself. Rather than viewing the Thessalonians as dry, brittle sponges needing to soak in the truth, Paul opened his heart and let them become dear to him. Instead of taking advantage, he worked day and night to avoid burdening them. Instead of living selfishly under a shallow gloss of spirituality, he modeled depth of character, like a father with his family.

32

That doesn't mean Paul was a pushover or a spiritual softie; he was a warrior for the gospel. But he balanced his battle cry with soothing whispers of grace.

A Contagious Style Is Relevant in Approach

Paul invested himself deeply in the Thessalonians so they would "walk in a manner worthy of the God who called them into His own kingdom and glory" (v. 12). His next words are revealing to us as well:

> And for this reason we also constantly thank God that when you received from us the word of God's message, you accepted it not as the word of men, but for what it really is, the word of God, which also performs its work in you who believe. (v. 13)

The Thessalonians accepted the Word of God because of its relevance. It scratched where they itched. It healed where they hurt. It made a difference in their lives (v. 13b). Paul knew their culture well, and he presented the gospel with the day's issues in mind. A church with a contagious style is *relevant in approach*.

We don't have to *make* the Scriptures relevant, they *are* relevant. We simply need to point out how relevant they are by holding them up against today's issues. We must serve the Scriptures on a plate with the fare *our* culture eats, not the stale leftovers from the sixties, fifties, or before.

Furthermore, we recognize the relevance of Scripture when we stop dividing the sacred from the secular. The Word of God is just as powerful trickling across the break room on Monday as it is flowing from the pulpit on Sunday. The way we conduct business, raise our children, or relate to our neighbor is no less sacred than the way we worship. Jesus saw no wall between the sacred and secular. He met beggars as beggars, politicians as politicians, prostitutes as prostitutes. Had he waited for them to come to worship, most of them never would have felt His healing touch.

A church with a contagious style is relevant; it meets people where they are.

When That Style Occurs . . .

Biblical in content. Authentic in nature. Gracious in attitude. Relevant in approach. What can we expect if we exercise all four of these characteristics?

- *From God.* We can expect Him to honor our efforts regardless of our weaknesses.

- *From ourselves.* We can expect to model Christlikeness with first-century zeal and twentieth-century style.

- *From others.* We can expect them to consider joining the fellowship in spite of the difficulties.

The secret to style is to keep the right perspective. We need more emphasis on content, less on cosmetics. More importance placed on depth, less on size. More interest in exalting Christ, less on spotlighting ourselves. More reminders that the church consists of people with eternal souls, not structures of tempered steel. More involvement with the lost outside our walls, not just the saved within. More delight in our relationship with God, fewer reminders of duty. More authenticity, less hypocrisy. More meaningful relationships, fewer lengthy meetings.

How about tossing another log on the fire?

 Living Insights STUDY ONE

As the bride of Christ, we are privileged to have an intimate relationship with our Groom. We love and worship Him. We're eternally united with Him. We bare our souls to Him. No one knows us better or loves us more faithfully than He does. As the marriage deepens, we have the joy of sharing Him with others. After all, how can a bride keep such happiness to herself?

Sometimes, though, we would rather remain in the refuge of the chapel than trudge down Main Street. We don't want to wrinkle our gown. Wedding dresses don't go with splattered mud or sleeping drunks. They snag on taxi doors. Escalators and revolving doors eat them for lunch. And just try stepping over a sidewalk grate in heels. But, as George MacLeod illustrates in his poem "Return the Cross to Golgotha," Main Street is exactly where the bride of Christ needs to be.

> I simply argue that the cross be raised again
>   at the center of the market place
>   as well as on the steeple of the church,
>
> I am recovering the claim that

Jesus was not crucified in a cathedral
between two candles:

But on a cross between two thieves;
on a town garbage heap;
At a crossroad of politics so cosmopolitan
that they had to write His title
in Hebrew and in Latin and in Greek . . .

And at the kind of place where cynics talk smut,
and thieves curse and soldiers gamble.

Because that is where He died,
and that is what He died about.
And that is where Christ's men ought to be,
and what church people ought to be about.[4]

How can we relate to the world around us if we don't know who's out there? Every now and then, we need to shed the gown, slip into some comfortable jeans, and meet the world on its own turf.

How about your local assembly? Is it sitting in the chapel waiting for guests to arrive, or is it passing out invitations in the street? Here are some questions to help you determine how well you're relating to your community:

Do all the ministries in your church take place at the church building?

_____

_____

Is your pastor considered a "professional evangelist," or do other members of the body reach out to the surrounding community?

_____

_____

Do you feel that most people in your local church are equipped to share their faith with others?

_____

4. George MacLeod, "Return the Cross to Golgotha," *Focal Point*, vol. 1 (January–March 1981).

35

Can you describe the square mile that surrounds your sanctuary—the streets, houses, lifestyles of the people?

_____

_____

_____

List the names of the neighbors on either side of you and across the street. When's the last time you had one of them over for dinner?

_____   _____

_____   _____

 Living Insights

Mannequins have never looked more alive. No longer imprisoned behind storefront glass, they're popping up (or is it propping up?) in areas of the store where one expects to see shoppers, not statues. Leaning against the second floor railing at J. C. Penney. Waiting for a friend by the escalator. Sitting in the shoe department, chin in hands. A svelte woman in a black skirt, her chestnut hair cascading over a scarlet jacket. A blonde man in khakis with a teal sweater slung over one shoulder. Giggling children in hot pursuit of a soccer ball. You might find yourself saying, "Excuse me" to one of them. They look so real. Until you get close.

Mannequins are designed to appear lifelike at a glance. But a closer look reveals their phoniness. God designed people differently. The closer others get to us, the more real we should be. Take Paul, for example. He knew he couldn't minister to the Thessalonians from a distance. So he let them get close enough to see his heart, his pain, his flaws.

How would you describe yourself? Real? Authentic? Or a mannequin Christian? Do you let others get close? Or do you prefer to keep them at a distance, hoping they'll be satisfied with a curious glance? Are you up-front with family, friends, and fellow believers? Or simply posing for them? Is the reality of Jesus Christ woven into your life's fabric? Or do you slip your spirituality on and off like a sport coat?

Give some thought to your personal authenticity. If anything comes to the surface that you'd like to change, write it down. Then make it a matter of prayer and practice.

Getting Real

_____

_____

_____

_____

_____

Chapter 5

THE DIFFERENCE BETWEEN A METROPOLITAN AND A NEIGHBORHOOD MENTALITY

Exodus 18:7–24; Ephesians 4:11–16

The widows were hungry.

The death of their husbands had left their hearts and stomachs empty. They had the spirit to work, but age and fatigue prevented it. Relatives couldn't support them; they had their own children to think of. So the widows turned to the church. Surely, He who fed thousands from a few loaves would provide bread through His apostles. And with so many new believers selling property and piling the profits at the apostles' feet, a miracle may not even be necessary. But whether by miracle or by money—it didn't matter. As long as the bread came.

The bread came all right. But not to the widows. The fledgling church, like a young mother overrun with children, had overlooked them. Feelings of neglect gnawed away at their hope, and the congregation grumbled with rumors. "The apostles are playing favorites," some growled. "Who do they think they are—deciding who eats and who doesn't?" "They would rather preach than pastor." "They're only interested in numbers; not individuals." Soon the complaints reached the apostles' ears. It was time to do something. But what?

The apostles' dilemma was clear: how to distribute food to the widows without neglecting their primary ministry of the Word and prayer? How to serve physical bread without skimping on spiritual bread? The solution was brilliant: Select faithful men from among the congregation to distribute the food. The widows ate. The body experienced the joy of serving one another. The teaching ministry of the apostles continued without interruption. And the church retained its reputation as a caring community (see Acts 6:1–7).

Oh, the irony of a flourishing ministry. The more God's hand moves in the church, causing spiritual and numerical growth, the more opportunities for people to slip through our fingers. The hungry widows in Acts 6 represent a whole list of challenges facing any thriving ministry, but especially a large metropolitan ministry: distributing resources, delegating responsibilities, understanding personal priorities, valuing people over programs, building a family instead of a corporation.

Scripture supplies principles for dealing with success as well as failure. So if you're feeling overwhelmed by the demands of a burgeoning ministry, this chapter might be just what you need.

Metropolitan Ministries: Neither New nor Novel

The big church has taken a bum rap in our day. For some of us, size alone makes a church suspect—which is interesting, considering that we view size as an asset for shopping malls, corporations, hospitals, and schools. For some reason, though, the large church with multiple ministries often conjures up images of an egocentric pulpiteer basking in the spotlight of a popular ministry. Such churches do exist. But big doesn't always mean bad.

Take the Jerusalem church, for example. More than five thousand members and growing by Acts 4:4. No electronic media. No high-powered pastor. No complex structure. Simply blessed by God in size and spirituality. Was it immune to problems? Certainly not, as the story of the hungry widows reveals. Even so, life-changing ministry thrived in this sprawling body of believers. Scripture suggests no aversion to a church merely because of its size.

Nor does history. As we flip through the church's photo album, pictures of large metropolitan ministries abound:

- Westminster Chapel in London—Led by G. Campbell Morgan for twenty-three years, then David Martyn Lloyd-Jones for thirty-two years.

- Metropolitan Tabernacle in London—Charles Haddon Spurgeon preached in this six-thousand-seat sanctuary that opened its doors when the Civil War began.

- First Baptist Church in downtown Dallas, Texas—an enormous congregation nurtured by George W. Truett and, later, W. A. Criswell.

- Moody Memorial Church in Chicago—where H. A. Ironside held forth.

- Tenth Presbyterian Church in Philadelphia—the great Donald

Barnhouse pastored here, succeeded by James Montgomery
Boice.

- Church of the Open Door in downtown Los Angeles—pastored
by several well-known expositors, including R. A. Torrey, Louis
T. Talbot, and J. Vernon McGee.

We could extend the list for several pages, but the point is clear:
large metropolitan churches are nothing new; they've been around
for a long time. And, since they're liable to be around for a few more
years, we would be wise to examine Scripture for principles that
will help us minister more effectively in a metropolitan context.

Timeless Principles for Staying Effective

Any how-to book on effective ministry would include interviews
with Moses and Paul. Both had hands-on experience with demand-
ing ministries. And both recorded principles that still apply today.

The Experience of Moses

Moses had acquired no ministry experience, except for forty
years of herding sheep in the desert. Then suddenly, at the ripe age
of eighty, he found himself recruited by God to pastor Wilderness
Bible Church, a congregation of about two million cantankerous
souls recently released from slavery. And the demands of ministry
engulfed him like a sandstorm. Fortunately, God sent him a
counselor—Jethro, his father-in-law—to help him cope with the
strain.

> And it came about the next day that Moses sat
> to judge the people, and the people stood about
> Moses from the morning until the evening. Now
> when Moses' father-in-law saw all that he was doing
> for the people, he said, "What is this thing that you
> are doing for the people? Why do you alone sit as
> judge and all the people stand about you from morn-
> ing until evening?" And Moses said to his father-in-
> law, "Because the people come to me to inquire of
> God. When they have a dispute, it comes to me,
> and I judge between a man and his neighbor, and
> make known the statutes of God and His laws." And
> Moses' father-in-law said to him, "The thing that
> you are doing is not good. You will surely wear out,

both yourself and these people who are with you, for the task is too heavy for you; you cannot do it alone."[1] (Exod. 18:13–18)

Moses was trapped on the treadmill of a one-man ministry. Driven by a desire to blend God's Law into the life of every Israelite, he was in danger of wearing out. The people were headed for exhaustion, too. Can you imagine waiting in line all day to see Moses?

Have you ever known a well-meaning pastor, elder, or counselor who has trouble delegating responsibility? Maybe you fit that description. If so, you know the frustration of trying to do it all yourself. Listen to Jethro's wise and loving admonition:

> "Now listen to me: I shall give you counsel, and God be with you. You be the people's representative before God, and you bring the disputes to God, then teach them the statutes and the laws, and make known to them the way in which they are to walk, and the work they are to do. Furthermore, you shall select out of all the people able men who fear God, men of truth, those who hate dishonest gain; and you shall place these over them, as leaders of thousands, of hundreds, of fifties and of tens. And let them judge the people at all times; and let it be that every major dispute they will bring to you, but every minor dispute they themselves will judge. So it will be easier for you, and they will bear the burden with you. If you do this thing and God so commands you, then you will be able to endure, and all these people also will go to their place in peace." (vv. 19–23)

Two key thoughts emerge from Jethro's counsel. The first is *communication*. Look again at verse 20, "Teach them the statutes and the laws." Remember the apostles' priority in Acts 6? The ministry of the Word. A leader who tries to pull every lever and grease every wheel in the ministry machine can't possibly maintain quality teaching.

The second idea is *delegation*. "Pass around the workload," Jethro

---

1. The Hebrew sentence is emphatic, beginning with the words *not good*: "Not good is the thing you are doing." John R. Kohlenberger III, *The Interlinear NIV Hebrew-English Old Testament* (Grand Rapids, Mich.: Zondervan Publishing House, 1987), p. 196.

urges. But not just to any warm body. Note the qualifications in verse 21: "able men who fear God, men of truth, those who hate dishonest gain." People of skill and character—that's who you put in charge. Divide the workload among them, then turn them loose.

Communicate. Delegate. Your load will lighten, and the work will get easier. And others will feel like a significant part of the ministry too. And the needs of the congregation will be met.

How does Moses' example specifically apply to a big, metropolitan ministry? In several ways: (1) we see that many people plus high expectations, multiplied by numerous needs equals *endless* responsibilities; (2) as the work of ministry increases, the load must be shifted—efficiency is sometimes revealed not in what we accomplish but in what we *relinquish;* and (3) God's servants are not exempt from the penalties of breaking God's natural laws. Too much work and not enough rest can make anyone ill, anxious, bitter, or broken.

The Perspective of Paul

Some may say that's just an Old Testament story; this idea of delegating isn't supported in the New. Why, that's really shirking responsibility! Hold on—not according to Paul.

> And He gave some as apostles, and some as prophets, and some as evangelists, and some as pastors and teachers, for the equipping of the saints for the work of service, to the building up of the body of Christ; until we all attain to the unity of the faith, and of the knowledge of the Son of God, to a mature man, to the measure of the stature which belongs to the fulness of Christ. As a result, we are no longer to be children, tossed here and there by waves, and carried about by every wind of doctrine, by the trickery of men, by craftiness in deceitful scheming; but speaking the truth in love, we are to grow up in all aspects into Him, who is the head, even Christ, from whom the whole body, being fitted and held together by that which every joint supplies, according to the proper working of each individual part, causes the growth of the body for the building up of itself in love. (Eph. 4:11–16)

Don't miss the three principles Paul packs into this passage.

First, *there are sufficient gifts to sustain any size church* (vv. 11–12). God gave spiritual gifts to His entire *body*, not just to the pastor. As long as there are people in the church, there are enough gifts to sustain the ministry.

Second, *when the gifts are exercised, congregations grow up* (vv. 13–14). A body must exercise all its parts to develop. The more Christians use their gifts, the more mature the body.

Third, *maximum involvement leads to healthy growth* (vv. 15–16). A church deepens spiritually as its members serve the Lord and one another. Spiritually sick congregations are often led by an over-committed pastor who sees himself as the only servant.

Understanding the Differences between Metropolitan and Neighborhood Ministries

Smaller neighborhood churches need the advice of Paul and Moses just as much as large churches with multiple staff and ministries do. However, the way Paul's and Moses' advice plays out will differ, as should our expectations of each kind of church. The following chart gives us a clearer picture of the differences between metropolitan and neighborhood mentalities and will, hopefully, alleviate some of the frustrations that so often plague these churches. Remember, one is not better than the other; they are each uniquely used by God.[2]

The "Neighborhood" Concept	The "Metropolitan" Concept
1. Close ties between pastor and people—"one big family . . . identifies with the pastor"	1. Close ties between identity groups—"numerous families . . . identify with one another"
2. Smaller scale: staff . . . vision . . . organization . . . facilities . . . budget . . . outreach . . . provision . . . variety	2. Large scale: staff . . . vision . . . organization . . . facilities . . . budget . . . outreach . . . provision . . . variety
3. Congregation drawn mainly from close radius	3. Congregation drawn from vast radius

2. This chart is taken from the book *The Bride: Renewing Our Passion for the Church*, by Charles R. Swindoll (Grand Rapids, Mich.: Zondervan Publishing House, 1994), p. 103 (page citation is to the second printing).

The "Neighborhood" Concept	The "Metropolitan" Concept
4. Tendency to be "inbred" . . . narrow rotation among lay leadership . . . greater reticence to change	4. Less "inbred" . . . broad rotation among lay leadership . . . less reticence to change
5. Easy to know everyone	5. Impossible to know everyone
6. Workload borne by volunteers	6. Some work delegated to specialists
7. Relatively simple to manage and maintain	7. Complex to manage and maintain
8. One-man operation . . . more rigid control	8. Multi-staff . . . team emphasis among all in leadership . . . broader base of control
9. Strong, centralized loyalty to "the church" . . . easier to implement involvement	9. Loyalty decentralized to various ministries . . . more difficult to implement involvement
10. Atmosphere naturally warm and friendly	10. Atmosphere can still be warm and friendly—but a constant challenge

Keep These Things in Mind . . .

As you contemplate the differences between a metropolitan and neighborhood mentality, keep these practical suggestions in mind.

- *If you have neighborhood expectations you will be frustrated in a metropolitan church.* The reverse is equally true.

- *Broad-minded flexibility and small-group participation are major secrets of survival for a healthy metropolitan church.* Expect change, and be open to a variety of ministry and music styles. And join a small group where you can build relationships.

- *Changing methods doesn't mean a changing message.* A church need not sacrifice biblical integrity on the altar of cultural relevance.

 *Living Insights*

When Benno Schmidt, Jr., assumed the presidency of Yale University, he expressed some fear about the demands of the job. He said, "If I can't put my feet on the desk and look out the window and think without an agenda, I may be managing Yale, but I won't be leading it."[3]

Many of us think managing and leading are the same thing, but they're different.

> "To manage" means "to bring about, to accomplish, to have charge of or responsibility for, to conduct." "Leading" is "influencing, guiding in direction, course, action, opinion." The distinction is crucial. *Managers are people who do things right and leaders are people who do the right thing.* The difference may be summarized as activities of vision and judgment— *effectiveness* versus activities of mastering routines— *efficiency.*[4]

Some churches, it seems, exist for one reason: to transform leaders into managers. Perhaps you've witnessed the metamorphosis or experienced it personally. The new senior pastor arrives with exciting plans for the future. He's energized with vision and a passion for preaching the Word and grounding new believers in the faith. Before long, though, he's spending all of his time juggling details and putting out fires. He becomes a holy bellhop, frantically rushing to answer every need that rings out from the congregation. Meetings, crisis counseling sessions, and visitation leave him little time for reflection and study. He throws sermons together in a panic on Saturday afternoon and seldom spawns a creative idea. The vision he came with is gone, obscured by a fog of endless busyness.

Are you in a position of leadership—pastor, parent, CEO, mentor? Are you leading or managing? When's the last time you propped your feet on the desk, had your secretary hold your calls (or switched on the answering machine), and thought deeply about your life and

---

3. As quoted by Swindoll, in the book *The Bride*, p. 91 (page citation is to the second printing).

4. Warren Bennis and Burt Nanus, *Leaders: The Strategies for Taking Charge* (New York, N.Y.: Harper and Row, Publishers, 1985), p. 21.

ministry? Consider this Living Insight a note of permission to do that. Carve out a few hours this week to jump off the treadmill. Get alone and think. Pray. Dream. Evaluate. Reorganize. Delegate. Make some deliberate changes. And start leading again.

 Living Insights

Jesus' ministry was in full swing in Capernaum. "The whole city had gathered at the door" to see Him, Mark 1:33 says. He healed many of the sick there and cast out demons. But, as always, He found time to break away and linger in the light of communion with His Father. The apostles, overwhelmed by the needs of the people, finally found Jesus and informed Him of the backlog. His response? "Let us go somewhere else to the towns nearby, in order that I may preach there also; for that is what I came out for" (v. 38).

Jesus Christ, the one person capable of a "one-man ministry," chose not to meet every need while He walked the earth. Purpose— that's what kept Him moving. He knew why He had come. He never allowed the dust of distractions to cloud His direction. He was always delivering His message; always moving toward the Cross.

Have you ever crafted a purpose statement for your life? It might be what you need to stay on track in this busy world. It will empower you to say no more often. And you'll gain the satisfaction of doing what God has called you to do. Give it a try. Keep it simple. The following questions will help.

What purpose has God defined for *all* Christians, regardless of gifts, interests, or background (see 1 Cor. 10:31)?

What do I do well? What do I love to do? When am I most fulfilled?

What do my experiences tell me about my skills, interests, and dreams?

_____

_____

How can God use my unique abilities for His glory?

_____

_____

My purpose statement (which can be refined and updated):

_____

_____

_____

_____

Chapter 6

WHAT CHANGES AND WHAT DOESN'T

Selected Scriptures

My, how times have changed.

Not too long ago, we started cars with the turn of a crank. Now they talk to us, reminding us to fasten the seat belt or turn off the headlights. A steady rain used to turn streets into mud. Today we speed down paved superhighways on special tires that channel water off the surface.

Before the porcelain bathtub, whole families took turns bathing in a No. 2 washtub . . . often without changing water. Where was Calgon to take you away when you needed it?

The telegraph at one time was on the cutting edge of technology. Nowadays we transact business with a pocket phone, carry a computer in our briefcase, and fax images to the other side of the world. Cash-spitting ATMs have practically made bank tellers obsolete. And it's no longer necessary to tiptoe through the library to conduct research. Just tap into their files with your PC.

We've come a long way in a short time. The first space shuttle, *Columbia*, lifted off only seventy-eight years after the Wright brothers' historic twelve-second flight. Fewer than one hundred years separate Thomas Edison's light bulb and laser surgery. And the atomic bomb exploded in Hiroshima just eighty years after Robert E. Lee's surrender at Appomattox. If that pace doesn't make your head spin, this vision of the future certainly will:

> In the year 2020, automobiles probably will be powered by an advanced battery pack for the short runs to and from offices and shopping. For the longer trips, cars will be powered by liquid-hydrogen engines. The exhaust from our future highway vehicles will be pure oxygen and steam, which are the by-products from burning liquid hydrogen. In effect, there will be tens of millions of rolling vacuum cleaners sucking the smog out of the cities and replacing it with air cleaner than the air above the

Colorado Rockies. A big semi-trailer will roar down the freeway, belching clouds of pure oxygen out of its stacks. There will be a sticker on the back of the truck with a new slogan: "Teamsters for Clean Air!"[1]

How can the church brace itelf for the winds of change? The first thing to do, according to the prophet Daniel, is realize that God is still in control.

> "And it is He who changes the times and the epochs;
> He removes kings and establishes kings;
> He gives wisdom to wise men,
> And knowledge to men of understanding."
> (Dan. 2:21)

"Don't be alarmed," says Daniel. God still calls the shots. Change doesn't scare Him, no matter how dizzying the pace is for us. In fact, nothing changes without His permission (see also Ps. 31:15a).

Modern accomplishments actually hold some thrilling implications for the communication of the gospel and the infusion of authentic Christianity into our world. The challenge for the bride of Christ is to flex with the times without faltering in her commitment. That takes a keen understanding of what changes and what stays the same.

Some Things Will Never Change

David grappled with the coexistence of the changing and the changeless. His life shaken by the tremors of Saul's relentless pursuit, David longed to stand once again on something solid.

> In the Lord I take refuge;
> How can you say to my soul, "Flee as a bird to
>   your mountain;
> For, behold, the wicked bend the bow,
> They make ready their arrow upon the string,
> To shoot in darkness at the upright in heart.
> If the foundations are destroyed,
> What can the righteous do?"
> (Ps. 11:1–3)

---

1. Dennis Waitley, *Ten Seeds of Greatness* (Old Tappan, N.J.: Fleming H. Revell Company, 1983), p. 167.

"Lord, I take refuge in You," says David. "You're my protector. But what can the righteous do if everything is up for grabs? Would You begin to change too? Then where could I go—what could I do?"

David's dilemma still exists today. How can the church stand firm when shock waves of change rattle our world? The apostle Paul answers that question in his second and final letter to Timothy. Writing from a prison cell in Rome just before his execution, Paul gives his friend and protégé rock-solid advice for shaky times.

> Remind them of these things, and solemnly charge them in the presence of God not to wrangle about words, which is useless, and leads to the ruin of the hearers. Be diligent to present yourself approved to God as a workman who does not need to be ashamed, handling accurately the word of truth. But avoid worldly and empty chatter, for it will lead to further ungodliness, and their talk will spread like gangrene. Among them are Hymenaeus and Philetus, men who have gone astray from the truth saying that the resurrection has already taken place, and thus they upset the faith of some. Nevertheless, the firm foundation of God stands, having this seal, "The Lord knows those who are His," and, "Let everyone who names the name of the Lord abstain from wickedness." (2 Tim. 2:14–19)

Trivial debates. Ungodliness. Spiritual desertion. False teaching. Just a few of the tremors pulsing through the church of Ephesus during Timothy's ministry there. Paul's exhortation? "Remind the congregation of the timeless truth of God's Word, Timothy. Some will try to pull you into verbal battles that have no purpose other than upsetting the flock. But stay focused on the main thing—the communication of God's unchanging truth" (see vv. 14–15).

Hymenaeus and Philetus, apparently members of the Ephesian church, had already demonstrated the dangers of straying from God's truth. By disregarding Scripture, they inflicted damage to the faith of other believers (vv. 16–18).

People will try to shake us up. God's Word, however, stands firm (v. 19a). And just so we'll remember that, He has provided assurance through a "seal" of His solidity in the lives of "those who are His" (v. 19b). In other words, the lifestyles of the righteous are proof of God's unchanging foundation.

How reassuring! We can live in the epicenter of change without crumbling, as long as we stand on the truth of God's holy Word.

Our challenge is to stay up with the times, to serve our generation, yet in no way alter the truths of Scripture. In a nutshell, *we must be willing to leave the familiar without disturbing the essentials.* The bride of Christ must keep up with current fashions without compromising her character.

Unfortunately, many evangelical churches have failed to meet this challenge. Afraid of change, they cling to yesterday's methodology as though it were as sacred as Scripture. They avoid any modern technique or invention, as if adopting them would be tantamount to tampering with the Bible. But God demands no such rigidity from His body. If fax machines, computers, and audio-visual presentations help advance the kingdom of God without compromising our theology or contaminating our message, why not use them?

At the same time, there are dangers in embracing something simply because it's new. Modern doesn't necessarily mean pure or godly. As we keep an attentive ear to new developments, let us not lose the voice of God in the clamor.

Listening to God becomes more important as our society advances. More than ever, as we adjust our lives to the times in which we live, we need to continue hearing what He is saying. Because, as 2 Timothy 3 tells us, the future church is in for some rough times.

> But realize this, that in the last days difficult times will come. For men will be lovers of self, lovers of money, boastful, arrogant, revilers, disobedient to parents, ungrateful, unholy, unloving, irreconcilable, malicious gossips, without self-control, brutal, haters of good, treacherous, reckless, conceited, lovers of pleasure rather than lovers of God; holding to a form of godliness, although they have denied its power. . . . Evil men and impostors will proceed from bad to worse, deceiving and being deceived.
> (2 Tim. 3:1–5a, 13)

The future, even with all its glittering advancements, will wear the tarnish of the same difficult experiences, depraved people, and deceitful practices that exist today. So to live effectively in the "last days," the church needs to follow God's voice more than any other. We must stay alert, informed, and anchored to His truth.

The Major Ingredient for Survival

What will it take to stay up with our times while standing firm on God's truth? In a word, *discernment*. Webster defines *discernment* as "the quality of being able to grasp and comprehend what is obscure."[2] We need to pay attention, ask questions, make wise choices. As the current of change takes us into the future, discernment will help us locate and negotiate the rapids of heresy.

Two Suggestions for Keeping Our Balance

Remember, our challenge is to leave the familiar—outdated methodology—without disturbing the essentials—the truth of God's Word. Here are two suggestions for maintaining that delicate balance.

First, *changing times require the willingness to retool and flex where needed.* We need to keep evaluating and rethinking our approach to ministry. Consider worship, for example. Would we be more in tune with our community by blending a few praise choruses with traditional hymns? Is one service per week enough? Are three too many? Should we develop a small-group program? How about the church office? Would fax machines and voice mail help us minister more effectively? Or should we stick with the answering machine? Which audio-visual tools can we use to enhance the way we teach the Scriptures and train people for evangelism?

Second, *changeless truths require the discipline to resist and fight when necessary.* Ministering in a changing world requires us to decide what's worth fighting for. Some of us would rather die than move the doxology from the beginning of the service to the end. But do we demonstrate the same passion when it comes to God's Word? The integrity of the Scriptures *is* worth fighting for. No amount of technological advancement gives us the right to tamper with God's everlasting truth. It is our firm foundation in changing times.

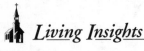 *Living Insights*

A charge to keep I have,
A God to glorify,

2. *Merriam Webster's Collegiate Dictionary*, 10th ed., see "discernment."

A never-dying soul to save,
And fit it for the sky.

To serve the present age,
My calling to fulfill,
Oh, may it all my pow'rs engage
To do my Master's will.[3]

Charles Wesley's hymn reveals the man's awareness of his times. He and his brother John ministered in "the present age" of eighteenth-century England, traveling thousands of miles on horseback to preach the Word to people who had no pastor or congregational family. Acutely aware that theology had become too dry and lofty for many laypeople, Charles crafted his thoughts not only into sermons but also into hymns. This was just one of the many vessels the Wesleys used to pour out the pure water of the Word on the diverse spiritual landscape of their day.

Are you in touch with *your* present age? Do you know the issues affecting the church and the world? Are you up with the times or lagging behind in "the good old days"? Don't look now, but some of us are guilty of answering questions people stopped asking years ago.

The good news is that it's never too late to learn. If you feel out of touch, take a couple of hours this week to catch up on your culture. Visit the library and peruse *Time* or *Newsweek*. Flip through a computer or business magazine. Take in a movie (a new one!). Or simply spend some time listening to your neighbor talk about the things that are important to him or her.

Then delve back into the Scriptures, asking God to help you live out His changeless truth in your changing world.

One new thing I learned about my world: _____

_____

_____

How do the Scriptures relate to what I've learned? _____

_____

_____

3. Charles Wesley, "A Charge to Keep I Have," in *New Songs of Inspiration* (Dallas, Tex.: Zondervan Corporation, Stamps-Baxter Music, 1982), vol. 8, no. 21.

What are the implications for my local church and personal ministry?_____

_____

_____

Living Insights

Spend a few minutes evaluating the ministries in your church. In the space provided, list the major activities you are involved in. Zero in on something that's been done the same way for a while. Is there a fresh way to accomplish this activity? For example, how about using an overhead projector or handouts for the Bible study instead of lecturing the whole hour? What's something unique to share with a hospital patient? How can some fun be injected into that dull budget meeting? Could the women's group meet somewhere different? Or the sermon begin with a short skit? How can neighbors be drawn more creatively into a discussion of spiritual matters?

_____

_____

_____

_____

_____

_____

Choose one idea and give it a whirl this week.

Chapter 7

MINISTERING IN THE LAST DAYS

2 Timothy 3; Matthew 24:3–12

Jesus never received an invitation to speak at the annual convention of the Society of Optimists.

When the Lord's disciples asked Him to paint a verbal picture of the final days before His return, He coated the canvas with the blacks and grays of a winter night. No wispy pastels of spring or rich autumn auburns. No summer yellows. Only the shadows of deceit, the smoke of conflict, and the glint of icy hearts.

> And as He was sitting on the Mount of Olives, the disciples came to Him privately, saying, "Tell us, when will these things be, and what will be the sign of Your coming, and of the end of the age?" And Jesus answered and said to them, "See to it that no one misleads you. For many will come in My name, saying, 'I am the Christ,' and will mislead many. And you will be hearing of wars and rumors of wars; see that you are not frightened, for those things must take place, but that is not yet the end. For nation will rise against nation, and kingdom against kingdom, and in various places there will be famines and earthquakes. But all these things are merely the beginning of birth pangs. Then they will deliver you to tribulation, and will kill you, and you will be hated by all nations on account of My name. And at that time many will fall away and will deliver up one another and hate one another. And many false prophets will arise, and will mislead many. And because lawlessness is increased, most people's love will grow cold." (Matt. 24:3–12)

Things will get worse—that's the bad news. The good news is that God is still in control. He watches the gathering darkness with eternal confidence. And at His appointed time, He will send the Lord Jesus Christ back to earth to claim His bride and rule as King of Kings.

Meanwhile, the church must minister in a world that grows colder and more hostile by the day. Though God will not allow the wind of the end times to snuff out the church's fire, He does want us to prepare for winter. That begins with some realistic expectations.

General Evaluation: What We Should Expect

Based on Jesus' forecast in Matthew 24, we can expect the coming winter to alter the world's spiritual scenery in three ways: first, conditions will worsen; second, homes will weaken; third, morals will wane.

Conditions Will Worsen

Jesus warns that nations will refuse to tolerate one another. Skirmishes will erupt around the planet as predatory regimes try to devour weaker countries. Sounds a lot like our day, doesn't it? Only a few years ago, troops from the United States and other countries spilled onto the sands of the Middle East to keep Saddam Hussein and his Iraqi army from consuming Kuwait. At the time of this writing, the war for "ethnic cleansing" still rages in Bosnia-Herzegovina. The democratic government of Haiti stands on wobbly legs after years of military rule. And the African nation of Rwanda festers from the carnage of intertribal hatred.

Bumper stickers urging us to "Visualize World Peace" will do little to weaken the winds of conflict. Though well-intentioned statesmen and women strive for international peace, its lasting presence will elude us until Christ's return.

Individuals will get along no better than nations. We'll continue to offend, abuse, and kill one another. More people than ever will succumb to internal conflict and commit suicide—perhaps even legally with the assistance of a physician.

Homes Will Weaken

Families will continue to disintegrate. Most of us know someone who's nursing the sting of a marital split. Perhaps you've even felt it yourself.

Same-sex "marriages" are going public. Emotional and physical abuse make the headlines every day. Absent or apathetic parents, peer pressure, and the media prompt our children to step out of the family circle and explore dangerous territory. Drive-by shootings and other gang-related crimes flash from the evening news with numbing frequency. Teachers with tenure are leaving their profession to escape rampant delinquency among students.

Once the cords that held society together, family ties are now fraying like a rope on a sharp rock.

Morals Will Wane

In 1939, a four-letter word uttered by Clark Gable at the end of *Gone with the Wind* made headlines. But it no longer makes us blush. Far more offensive words and images skip into our consciousness through television, radio, movies, music, print, and other media. You can even buy subscriptions to X-rated computer programs. As technology advances, so will the options for perversity.

Even the ministry, which once had the sheen of a respectable profession, today wears the tarnish of men and women who exploit the name of Jesus Christ for money, fame, and power. And they will continue. As the waves of temptation crash against the church, pastors and parishioners alike will compromise their integrity and drift from their godly moorings.

That's a pretty bleak forecast. You might be thinking, as James Russell Lowell wrote, "Truth forever on the scaffold, Wrong forever on the throne."[1] But remember, as we saw in our previous chapter, God's foundation will stand against the storm (see 2 Tim. 2:19). His truth will prevail. The question, then, for the church is, How do we live and minister in a world that has lost its way?

Scriptural Instruction: How We Must Respond

Second Timothy 3 contains one of the most vivid accounts in the Bible of spiritual decay—but it also gives us the practical steps to face it.

A Brief Exposé of Last-Days' Depravity

> But realize this, that in the last days difficult times will come. (2 Tim. 3:1)

Paul begins by cautioning his longtime friend Timothy to stay alert. "Realize that the tough times are here to stay, Timothy. Wake up! Don't expect the storm to blow over."

---

1. James Russell Lowell, as quoted in *12,000 Religious Quotations*, comp. Frank S. Mead (1965; reprint, Grand Rapids, Mich.: Baker Book House, 1989), p. 452.

The Greek term Paul uses for *difficult* appears only one other time in Scripture—in Matthew 8:28. There it's translated *exceedingly violent* to describe two demon-possessed men. Our word *savage* might be more descriptive. If you don't believe we live in savage times, just scan the headlines:

- Mother Drowns Her Two Children
- Famous Athlete Arrested for Double Murder
- Man Murders Family, Friends; Hides Bodies
- Disgruntled Employee Shoots Boss
- Baby Thrown from Third-Story Window
- Doctor Assists in Another Suicide

"Don't gloss over what's happening," says Paul. Thinking positively won't help. Thinking *realistically* will.

He continues with piercing specificity.

> For men will be lovers of self, lovers of money, boastful, arrogant, revilers, disobedient to parents, ungrateful, unholy, unloving, irreconcilable, malicious gossips, without self-control, brutal, haters of good, treacherous, reckless, conceited, lovers of pleasure rather than lovers of God; holding to a form of godliness, although they have denied its power; and avoid such men as these. For among them are those who enter into households and captivate weak women weighed down with sins, led on by various impulses, always learning and never able to come to the knowledge of the truth. And just as Jannes and Jambres opposed Moses, so these men also oppose the truth, men of depraved mind, rejected as regards the faith. (2 Tim. 3:2–8)

As you hover over that passage, let your eyes light on a few key words.

Irreconcilable (v. 3). More and more offenses will go unforgiven. Your neighbor won't let you forget that you accidentally nipped his begonias with your mower. Or you may never get a chance to speak with the guy who slipped and fell in your store, but you'll hear from his attorney.

Jannes and Jambres (v. 8). These were the magicians in Pharaoh's court who attempted to mock God by imitating His power (see Exod. 7:10–12). People will be like them, says Paul—not only ignoring the truth but aggressively opposing it.

Depraved mind (2 Tim. 3:8). These enemies of the truth will be corrupt in their consciences and rejected by God.

Ready for some *good* news?

> But they will not make further progress; for their
> folly will be obvious to all, as also that of those two
> [Jannes and Jambres] came to be. (v. 9)

With that little word *but*, it's as if Paul puts his arm around Timothy's shoulder and reassures, "Don't worry, Timothy. Some of God's people will resist attacks on the truth. They will see through the veneer of phony religion, refusing to get sucked into the system. In the winter of the last days, the flame of God's truth will not die." How encouraging!

Wise Answers to All Who Minister

So how do we keep the fire burning? How do we survive these last days? The apostle gives us four practical answers. We'll look at two now, and save the last two for chapter 8.

First, *follow the model of the faithful.*

> But you followed my teaching, conduct, purpose,
> faith, patience, love, perseverance, persecutions, and
> sufferings, such as happened to me at Antioch, at
> Iconium and at Lystra; what persecutions I endured,
> and out of them all the Lord delivered me! And
> indeed, all who desire to live godly in Christ Jesus
> will be persecuted. (2 Tim. 3:10–12)

The word *follow* here means to "follow what has been grasped." Dr. Luke uses the term in Luke 1:3 to describe his "investigation" of the facts of Jesus' life.[2] The word connotes close observation and understanding.

"You've studied my life, Timothy," says Paul, "and found me to be faithful. Now follow my example and you'll make it." The godly

2. Gerhard Kittel and Gerhard Friedrich, eds., *Theological Dictionary of the New Testament*, trans. Geoffrey W. Bromiley (Grand Rapids, Mich.: William B. Eerdmans Publishing Co., 1985), p. 34.

examples of others will help us minister in the last days.

Second, *return to the truth of the past.*

> But evil men and impostors will proceed from bad to worse, deceiving and being deceived. You, however, continue in the things you have learned and become convinced of, knowing from whom you have learned them; and that from childhood you have known the sacred writings which are able to give you the wisdom that leads to salvation through faith which is in Christ Jesus. (vv. 13–15)

"Remember your roots, Timothy." Paul reminds Timothy of his rich spiritual heritage—the faith passed on from his mother and grandmother (see 2 Tim. 1:5).

You may be blessed with a strong spiritual lineage. If so, don't forget it. Review it, thank God for it. Anchor yourself deeply in the truths that have endured throughout time, and you will endure the bluster of the last days.

 Living Insights STUDY ONE

Picture your spiritual family tree. Where does your name hang? Near the top, on one of the newest branches? Are you a spry, young leaf dangling above the previous generations? Or maybe you're the trunk—providing support for all the branches that have sprouted from your legacy of faith. Or the roots—old, deep, unnoticed—but firmly fixed in the soil of faith, drinking in the Word and passing it on. Or perhaps you're a tender sapling in the early stages of growth—the first in your family to come to faith in Christ.

Wherever you fit on the tree, your spiritual life connects with someone else's. You've either influenced another by your walk with God, or you've been influenced. Probably both.

Think of someone on your tree with whom you'd like to strengthen your connection. Who is it? A grandfather who told you about Jesus on a fishing trip? Your mother, whose walk with God has stayed as reliable and unpretentious as a faded apron? Maybe a discouraged daughter needs to know the Christian life is still worth living. How about that brother who's fed up with Christians talking one way and living another?

Take a few minutes to write that person a letter. If he or she has helped nourish you spiritually, make it a letter of thanks. If the individual looks to you for growth, craft a note of encouragement and personal interest. We'll help you get started.

Name and relationship: _____

Specific ways he or she has nourished me, or specific things I would like him or her to absorb from my life: _____

_____

_____

_____

_____

Other things I want to cover: _____

_____

_____

_____

_____

 Living Insights _____ STUDY TWO

Do you ever wonder if truth goes out of style? With so many doctrinal fads parading before the church, maybe treasuring the truth seems foolish—like stockpiling bell bottoms and leisure suits. We hope this study is convincing you that God's truth, though it never changes, is always up to date. And it's still the most important garment in our spiritual closet. John R. W. Stott tells us why.

> We sometimes get distressed in our day—rightly and understandably—by the false teachers who oppose the truth and trouble the church, especially by the sly and slippery methods of backdoor religious traders. But we need have no fear, even if a few weak people may be taken in, even if falsehood becomes fashionable. For there is something patently spurious about heresy, and something self-evidently true about the truth. Error may spread and be popular for

a time. But it "will not get very far." In the end it is bound to be exposed, and the truth is sure to be vindicated. This is a clear lesson of church history. Numerous heresies have arisen, and some have seemed likely to triumph. But today they are largely of antiquarian interest. God has preserved his truth in the church.[3]

Just in case you're ever tempted to ditch the truth for a more stylish ensemble, write down three biblical truths that you believe in with unwavering conviction, along with any supporting Scripture references. Commit them to memory; carry them with you if necessary. Don't worry. They won't wear out.

Truth 1: _____

_____

Scripture references: _____

_____

Truth 2: _____

_____

Scripture references: _____

_____

Truth 3: _____

_____

Scripture references: _____

_____

3. John R. W. Stott, *Guard the Gospel: The Message of 2 Timothy* (Downers Grove, Ill.: InterVarsity Press, 1973), p. 91.

Chapter 8

"STAYIN' READY 'TIL QUITTIN' TIME"

2 Timothy 3:10–4:8

If you've ever worked on the floor of a factory or machine shop, you know that one thing rules your routine—the whistle. After you punch the time clock in the morning, your shift begins with an ear-splitting blast that shatters any lingering sleepiness from the night before. Another shrill cry at noon signals the lunch hour. And the five o'clock shriek? Well, that means quitting time. Shut down the machines and head for the shower, where another day's worth of grease and sweat melt away under the warm whispers of the water.

After a few years on the job, you can set your watch by that whistle. You can even predict the blast seconds before it goes off. And you learn to "stay ready 'til quittin' time." In shoptalk that means you remain hard at work while eagerly anticipating the final whistle.

You might say the church is hard at work on the earth's factory floor. God keeps us here to radiate His glory and communicate His gospel until quittin' time—the return of the Lord Jesus Christ. But a routine whistle blast won't signal His coming. He'll arrive with sudden and unprecedented spectacle.

> For the Lord Himself will descend from heaven with a shout, with the voice of the archangel, and with the trumpet of God; and the dead in Christ shall rise first. Then we who are alive and remain shall be caught up together with them in the clouds to meet the Lord in the air, and thus we shall always be with the Lord. (1 Thess. 4:16–17)

Are you stayin' ready 'til quittin' time? Serving the Lord while joyfully anticipating His return? Or will the trumpet blast catch you by surprise? Most of us, unfortunately, don't live with the day-to-day expectancy of Christ's return. Maybe we can change that by studying the Gospels more personally, which tell us He could come at *any* moment.

A Few Predictions from Jesus' Life

During His earthly ministry, Jesus often cautioned His disciples to prepare for His second coming. In Matthew 24 He urged them to "be on the alert," for, like a thief in the night, "the Son of Man is coming at an hour when you do not think He will" (see vv. 42–44).

Mark's gospel echoes this refrain: "Take heed, keep on the alert" (13:33). For Christ will not only come with the unexpectedness of a burglar, He will return as One who has entrusted His house to our care (vv. 34–37). He might come before the sun burns away the morning mist, in the heat of noonday, or in the cool stillness of a star-sprayed night. Jesus' point is: we must be about His work as though today were the day.

"Be on guard," Jesus stresses again in Luke, but this time with a slightly different slant:

> "that your hearts may not be weighted down with
> dissipation and drunkenness and the worries of life,
> and that day come on you suddenly like a trap." (21:34)

With minds and hearts staggering under the world's crushing load, we can be so preoccupied that Christ's return will suddenly spring shut on us like a trap. So Jesus says to stay alert! Stay focused through prayer! Then we'll be ready when He comes (vv. 35–36).

Finally, in the gospel of John, Jesus gently urges "let not your heart be troubled" but rather be encouraged, because His second coming means that we'll be with Him forever in a place He's personally prepared for us (14:1–3). Our alert, on-guard readiness needn't come from frantic fear but from the peace we have from knowing we're loved and wanted by God.

> "These things I have spoken to you, that in Me you
> may have peace. In the world you have tribulation,
> but take courage; I have overcome the world." (16:33)

Knowing that Jesus would overcome death itself and someday return to take them home, the disciples could go on ministering in the midst of intense persecution. They stayed ready 'til quittin' time. And so can we.

Specific Principles from Paul's Pen

In our previous study, we began to look at four principles in 2 Timothy for living and ministering in the last days. We got as far as the first two—do you remember them?

First, *follow the model of the faithful* (2 Tim. 3:10–12). Paul told Timothy, "You've studied my life and found me to be faithful. Now follow my example." Likewise, we gain encouragement from men and women who model an authentic walk with God.

Second, *return to the truth of your past* (vv. 13–15). Paul reminded Timothy to treasure the rich spiritual heritage passed on from his mother and grandmother. By connecting with our spiritual roots, we anchor ourselves for ministry in the last days. But what about those who come to Christ apart from such a lineage? They are no less equipped for last days' ministry, since they possess the inspired Word of God (vv. 16–17).

Now let's turn our attention to the final chapter of 2 Timothy. In fact, it's the final chapter of Paul's life. With his execution looming, the great apostle passes the torch to his young friend. His last words provide two more practical principles for ministering in light of the Lord's imminent return.

Proclaim the Message of Christ

> I solemnly charge you in the presence of God and of Christ Jesus, who is to judge the living and the dead, and by His appearing and His kingdom: preach the word; be ready in season and out of season; reprove, rebuke, exhort, with great patience and instruction. (2 Tim. 4:1–2)

"Preach the Word, Timothy." Paul's exhortation makes sense. After all, Timothy *is* a preacher. But the principle applies to all believers, because communicating the message of Jesus Christ is *our* duty and privilege too.

Three qualities of communication rise to the surface of Paul's charge to Timothy. First, *urgency*—"Be ready," Paul says. Rather than scrambling for the Word when we need it, we should have it poised for delivery (see also 1 Pet. 3:15).

There is also *consistency*—"in season and out of season." In other words, when it's convenient and when it's not. When others are open, when they are closed. When we feel good, when we feel bad. If the weather's cold, windy, hot, or humid. At home or at work. When we're appreciated, when we're resented. Whether it's permitted by the authorities or forbidden. The Word must flow with consistency, not stagnate in a pond of apathy, fear, or mismanaged priorities.

By the way, we can't take Paul's counsel as a warrant for rudeness. We need not abandon tact and respect for the sake of consistency. If our hearts and minds are brimming with the Word of God, the gospel will flow naturally at the appropriate time.

Notice, too, that the Word should be offered with *simplicity*. There's nothing sophisticated about verse 2 of 2 Timothy 4: "Reprove, rebuke, exhort, with great patience and instruction." No complex philosophies or lofty theories here. "Just take this body of truth," says Paul, "and declare it. Take the groceries of God's Word and feed the spiritually hungry." Why make the truth clang with complexity when it sings with simplicity? Just peruse the proverbs of Solomon and the parables of Jesus. So simple, yet so piercingly profound.

Maintain an Exemplary Life

There is a fourth and final principle for stayin' ready 'til quittin' time: *Maintain an exemplary life*.

> For the time will come when they will not endure sound doctrine; but wanting to have their ears tickled, they will accumulate for themselves teachers in accordance to their own desires; and will turn away their ears from the truth, and will turn aside to myths. But you, be sober in all things, endure hardship, do the work of an evangelist, fulfill your ministry. (2 Tim. 4:3–5)

The closer we get to Christ's return, the more teachers will tickle people's fancy, telling them what they *want* to hear instead of what they *need* to hear. Knowing that Timothy will be tempted to do the same, Paul issues four commands for teaching and living God's truth.

Be sober in all things. Stay calm and sane, he advises, even when we're tempted to embellish our ministry with clever novelties and cute fads. There's nothing wrong with creativity—until it becomes compromise.

Endure hardship. The sirens of heresy will always try to entice us to a "safe haven" that actually steers us into the rocks. But stay with your original course, urges Paul, no matter how much you're battered by the winds and waves of hardship. Plot a slow, steady course of doctrinal purity, and don't deviate from it.

Do the work of an evangelist. Keep speaking and living Christ's message of salvation. The best way to counteract phony gospels is with a steady supply of the truth.

Fulfill your ministry. Standing strong against the tempest of unsound doctrine will enable each of us to serve Christ to the fullest in whatever ministry He designs for us.

Timeless Facts That Maintain Our Readiness

Where do we go from here? How do we minister while keeping our ears perked for the final trumpet? Paul has just a few more words of advice.

> For I am already being poured out as a drink offering, and the time of my departure has come. I have fought the good fight, I have finished the course, I have kept the faith; in the future there is laid up for me the crown of righteousness, which the Lord, the righteous Judge, will award to me on that day; and not only to me, but also to all who have loved His appearing. (vv. 6–8)

In Paul's emotional reflection, we find three steps for stayin' ready 'til quittin' time.

First, *consider your life an offering to God rather than a monument to people.* Paul thought of himself as a drink offering, poured out for God's glory. He wasn't obsessed with polishing his image. Monuments crumble. Images fade. But an offering is an act of worship that honors our eternal heavenly Father.

Second, *remember that finishing well is the final proof that the truth works.* Anyone can start the Christian life with a bang. But walking with God is a marathon, not a sprint. When the race is over, what really counts is how we finish. That's why Paul could say with confidence, "I have fought the good fight, I have finished the course, I have kept the faith."

Third, *fix your eyes on the rewards of heaven rather than the allurements of earth.* A crown is coming for every person who loves and serves Christ. But don't look for it in this life. Satisfaction and recognition lie beyond the temporary trophies of this planet. Though eternal rewards come later, they never tarnish.

Follow the model of the faithful. Return to the truth of your past. Proclaim the message of Christ. Maintain an exemplary life. And you'll always be ready for quittin' time—when the Groom returns for His bride.

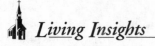

It's midnight. You're nestled under the covers, warmly enfolded in the arms of slumber. Gently, imperceptibly at first, sounds from the outside world trickle into your sleep. Music? Singing, perhaps. Or voices. Maybe all three. As the fog of unconsciousness begins to lift, the noises evaporate. But there's something else. A light— piercing white—burning away the last stubborn layer of sleep. You're awake now; this is no dream.

Fear fastens to your heart like a grappling hook and yanks you to an upright position. Across the room, standing in a swirling cloud of light, is . . . an angel. After allowing you to catch your breath, he introduces himself. When the shock finally wears off, you become convinced of his authenticity. He has been dispatched to let you in on the exact time of the Lord's return. It will be tomorrow at midnight, twenty-four hours from now. Then, with a rush of heavenly music, he disappears. You stare at the space he occupied, your eyes focused on the faint ghost of his image and your mind frantic with questions spawned by this splendid revelation.

What would you do for the next twenty-four hours? The only thing you know for sure is that you wouldn't sleep! Should you assemble the family and wait? Read the Bible, sing hymns, and pray until the Master comes? Should you bang on doors and share the gospel until you drop? Maybe it's time to forgive the friend who hurt you. Or write a love note to your spouse. Or reconcile with your teenager. Should you desperately try to get your spiritual life back on track, so the Lord will find you ready? Perhaps you should pray for more time.

What would you do? Think about it. Write down your answers.

_____

_____

_____

One more question. Are you doing any of those things now? None of us will ever receive twenty-four-hour's notice from an angel. But Christ could come at any time. Do you live with a sense of urgency that compels you to spend each day as though it might be your last on earth? Do you need to do some spiritual housecleaning before the Master returns? Write down one thing you would like to straighten up before Jesus comes back. Give it some prayerful attention this week. And remember, this could be the day!

 Living Insights STUDY TWO

German Silva finished well. But it wasn't easy. The twenty-six-year-old runner from Mexico took a wrong turn in the 1994 New York City Marathon—less than one mile from the finish line. After a police officer waved him back on course, Silva had to scramble to overtake his friend and training partner, Benjamin Paredes. Silva won with a time of two hours, eleven minutes, and twenty-one seconds—only two seconds ahead of Paredes. It was the closest finish in the history of the race.

We also make wrong turns in the Christian life, don't we? Even Paul, the great apostle who ran with unwavering vigor, admitted that his race was less than perfect (see Rom. 7:7–25; 1 Tim. 1:15). But he still finished well. And so can we. Wrong turns need not keep us from completing the race. Satan would love to see us give up when we swerve into the side streets of failure and frustration. But we don't have to quit. We're accompanied by the Holy Spirit, the Word of God, and the church of Jesus Christ—each one energized with eternal endurance.

Have you taken any wrong turns lately? Maybe you're just weary and need some encouragement to keep going. Let God know about it. Ask His Spirit to give comfort and strength for the next leg of the race. Stop and refresh yourself in the shade of Scripture. Let one or more of the following passages blow across your brow:

> Psalm 37:23–24
> 2 Corinthians 12:9–10
> Isaiah 40:27–29
> Hebrews 12:1–3
> 1 Corinthians 9:24–27

Don't be afraid to ask the body of Christ for help if you're off course either—we're in this race together. Whatever you do, don't quit.

See you at the finish line.

Chapter 9

THE VALUE OF INTEGRITY

Selected Scriptures

Tuesday morning, January 28, 1986.

The temperature at Cape Canaveral dipped enough to cause concern among NASA engineers and technicians, who feared the chill might endanger the launch of the space shuttle *Challenger*. But bad weather had already caused a three-day delay. Influential executives and image-conscious bureaucrats were itching for a launch—more delays would mean bad press for NASA. Besides, *Challenger* was scheduled to reach space prior to President Reagan's State of the Union address, which would air that evening.

Despite protests by technical personnel, the countdown continued. At 11:38 A.M. *Challenger* streaked into the sky. Among the proud spectators was the family of Christa McAuliffe—a New Hampshire school teacher and the first ordinary citizen to join a space mission.

One minute and fourteen seconds later, ten miles above the earth, the unthinkable happened. As *Challenger's* main engines surged to full power, the craft exploded into an orange fireball. Tentacles of white smoke shot out in every direction, hurling hunks of flaming metal into the atmosphere. The sky rained debris for a full hour. As a horrified America watched, exuberant applause melted into stunned silence. The *Challenger* and her crew of seven were gone.

Later, technical experts pinpointed the cause of the explosion. A faulty seal called an O-ring allowed hot gases to escape and ignite the fuel. An investigation revealed that NASA engineers had warned management about the inferior seals a year earlier. But construction of the *Challenger* and plans for her launch went forward. It was determined that low temperatures on launch day further weakened the O-ring.

The *Challenger* tragedy began long before the explosion. It started not just in the construction of the shuttle but in the character of the people who ignored the repeated warnings of experts. It started with a smoldering breach of integrity.

A Crisis of Integrity

When integrity breaks down, the results are devastating. If you need a reminder of that fact, just look around.

- We no longer trust many elected officials—they embezzle funds, solicit sexual favors, and accept bribes.

- A crisis of sexual integrity is sabotaging marriages and snuffing out lives. The divorce rate continues to climb. Abortion claims the lives of 1.6 million babies a year.[1] And more than 160,000 people had died of AIDS by the end of 1993.[2]

- Financial integrity is waning too, as evidenced by stories of insider trading and price fixing. People cheat on their taxes without a twinge of remorse.

- Even the ministry, a profession expected to reflect the character of God Himself, counts money-hungry deceivers and sexual offenders among its ranks.

Dishonesty, corruption, and infidelity are eating away at the protective seal of society—with explosive results.

Integrity: There Is No Substitute

To patch up our integrity, we first need to know precisely what the term means and involves. Webster defines *integrity* as "an uncompromising adherence to a code of moral, artistic, or other values: utter sincerity, honesty, and candor: avoidance of deception, expediency, artificality, or shallowness of any kind."[3] This idea of completeness or wholeness is also at the root of the Hebrew term for *integrity* (as in Ps. 78:72).[4]

Integrity applies not only to what we think and believe but also to what we do. Ted Engstrom simply defines it as "doing what you

1. As cited by J. Carl Laney, "A Biblical Appraisal of the Abortion Epidemic," in *Living Ethically in the Nineties*, ed. J. Kerby Anderson (Wheaton, Ill.: Scripture Press Publications, Victor Books, 1990), p. 204.

2. John Ankerberg and John Weldon, *The Myth of Safe Sex* (Chicago, Ill.: Moody Press, 1993), p. 75.

3. *Merriam-Webster's New International Dictionary*, 3rd ed., see "integrity."

4. Francis Brown, S. R. Driver, and Charles A. Briggs, *The New Brown, Driver, Briggs, Gesenius Hebrew and English Lexicon* (Peabody, Mass.: Hendrickson Publishers, 1979), p. 1070.

said you would do."[5] In other words, keeping your promises.

A car dealer, lamenting the dearth of honesty he saw in his profession, said in one of his radio ads, "If you tell the truth, you don't have to remember nearly as much." Integrity means we don't have to concoct cover-ups. When the white light of scrutiny comes on, we can turn to face it, instead of scampering for the shadows.

Biblical Examples of Integrity

The word *integrity* appears some twenty-seven times in Scripture and only in the Old Testament. But biblical illustrations of integrity abound, even when the word itself is not used. Joseph, for example, wielded integrity as a defense against the relentless sexual advances of Potiphar's wife (see Gen. 39). During a time when speaking for God was sheer suicide, Elijah called Ahab a sinner to his face and challenged the prophets of Baal to a duel (1 Kings 18:16–19). Nathan's courage and honesty enabled him to look adulterous David in the eye and say, "You are the man" (2 Sam. 12:1–14).

When John the Baptizer's ministry was overshadowed by the Messiah's, he demonstrated his integrity with one statement, "He must increase, but I must decrease" (John 3:26–30). Stephen's commitment to the truth cost him his life at the hands of the Sanhedrin (Acts 6:8–7:60). When the Jewish Council ordered the apostles to stop preaching the gospel, Peter responded boldly, "We must obey God rather than men" (Acts 5:27–29). That's integrity!

And what about the prophet Daniel? Because of Daniel's excellent character, King Darius was about to promote him to the heights of power and position. Daniel's peers, however, jealous of his favor with the king and his squeaky-clean reputation, devised a plan that would make his integrity his downfall. Knowing that Daniel prayed faithfully three times a day, they tricked the king into making prayer illegal. Then they approached the king with their findings.

> "Daniel, who is one of the exiles from Judah, pays no attention to you, O king, or to the injunction which you signed, but keeps making his petition three times a day." Then, as soon as the king heard this statement, he was deeply distressed and set his

5. Ted W. Engstrom with Robert C. Larson, *Integrity* (Waco, Tex.: Word Books, 1987), p. 10.

mind on delivering Daniel; and even until sunset he kept exerting himself to rescue him. Then these men came by agreement to the king and said to the king, "Recognize, O king, that it is a law of the Medes and Persians that no injunction or statute which the king establishes may be changed." (Dan. 6:13–15)

So into the lions' den Daniel went. But just as Daniel stood by his commitment to God, so God stood by Daniel and kept him from harm. God delivered him; and the lions had his accusers for lunch instead. Whether tempted by the kiss of prosperity or threatened by the jaws of adversity, Daniel's integrity stood strong.

We could fill several pages with biblical examples of integrity, including the Lord Jesus Himself. But don't get the wrong idea— you don't have to be a prophet, martyr, or apostle to have integrity. It throbs quietly and consistently within the hearts of everyday people, emerging occasionally as a tender touch, a kept promise, an honest answer, an act of obedience, and in a thousand other nonspectacular ways. Integrity is for everyone.

Abiding Principles We Need to Remember

To help work this kind of integrity into our lives, let's package what we've studied into three memorable principles.

First, *true integrity implies that we do what is right even when no one is looking or when everyone is compromising.* True integrity cannot be faked, especially in the ministry. It's not just a convenient prop; it comes from within. Integrity doesn't fade when we walk from the pulpit to the prayer closet or from the boardroom to the bedroom. Nor does it fluctuate with the mercurial character of others. True integrity ignores the excuse, "Everyone else is doing it," and does what it knows is right.

Second, *real integrity stays in place whether the test is adversity or prosperity.* Integrity means that neither a promotion nor a demotion changes us. If the business prospers, we praise God and enjoy His blessing. If the company goes belly-up, we don't participate in shady deals to get the blessing back. Integrity survives a growing ministry or one that's struggling. It stays faithful when the marriage sails along effortlessly and when it hits a reef. Win or lose, pass or fail, real integrity lasts.

Third, *broken moral integrity means the spiritual leader forfeits the right to lead.* This principle may sound harsh or unforgiving, but according to Scripture, God not only expects more from leaders, He considers them unfit to lead when they fall into immorality. The only leader in the Bible who came close to maintaining his position after a severe breach of morality is David. Careful study, however, reveals that after committing adultery with Bathsheba, David never again enjoyed the full measure of God's blessing.

The Scriptures treat gross moral failure, especially sexual sin, as a unique category worthy of special attention:

> The one who commits adultery with a woman is
>   lacking sense;
> He who would destroy himself does it.
> Wounds and disgrace he will find,
> And his reproach will not be blotted out.
> (Prov. 6:32–33)

> Flee immorality. Every other sin that a man commits
> is outside the body, but the immoral man sins against
> his own body. (1 Cor. 6:18)

Add to these Paul's requirement that leaders be "above reproach" (1 Tim. 3:2), and it's easy to see why sexual sin among Christian leaders demands more than a casual response.

Does this mean the pastor who runs off with his secretary has drifted beyond the reach of God's forgiveness? Certainly not. But the pulpit is no place for a leader who disregards God's Word and betrays the trust of the flock. Moral failure usually reveals a deep character flaw in need of repair. That's where the restorative ministry of the church comes in. Spiritual mending after a fall occurs best in a clinic of loving confrontation and accountability, not in the arena of public ministry.

The Essential Value of Accountability

A. W. Tozer once said, "An ineffective, half-alive minister is a better advertisement for hell than a good man dead."[6] We need more shining examples of Christ and fewer walking billboards for the enemy. Paul knew this when he said, "I buffet my body and make it my slave, lest possibly, after I have preached to others, I

---

6. A. W. Tozer, *God Tells the Man Who Cares* (Camp Hill, Pa.: Christian Publications, 1992), p. 90.

myself should be disqualified" (1 Cor. 9:27).

Buffeting our bodies—maintaining integrity by keeping our passions in check—calls for a one-two punch. First, we need to lead with the left jab of self-analysis; time alone with God is crucial. But that's only half the combination. We need to follow with the right cross of personal accountability. Here's why:

> Being creatures with blind spots and tendencies toward rationalization, we must also be in close touch with a few trustworthy individuals with whom we meet on a regular basis. Knowing that such an encounter is going to happen helps us hold the line morally and ethically. I know of nothing more effective for maintaining a pure heart and keeping one's life balanced and on target than being a part of an accountability group. It is amazing what such a group can provide to help us hold our passions in check![7]

Religious Lone Rangers make easy targets for Satan's arrows. Let's stay accountable. And keep integrity intact.

 Living Insights STUDY ONE

> One can acquire anything in solitude except
> character.   —Stendahl[8]

Are you accountable? Is there someone in your life to whom you've given permission and ample opportunity to ask direct questions? If not, you might be setting yourself up for a fall. But it's never too late to start practicing accountability.

Give some prayerful consideration to someone who would make a good accountability partner—an individual who loves you and wants the best for you but isn't afraid to probe and confront when necessary. If you're a pastor, maybe the best person to approach is a friend who shepherds another church. He doesn't even have to

---

7. Charles R. Swindoll, from the book *The Bride: Renewing Our Passion for the Church* (Grand Rapids, Mich.: Zondervan Publishing House, 1994), p. 182 (page citation is to the second printing).

8. Swindoll, *The Bride*, p. 172, quoting Martin E. Marty, "Truth: Character in Context," *Los Angeles Times*, 20 December 1987, sec. 5, p. 1, col. 1 (page citation is to the second printing).

live in the same town. If you're a businessperson, perhaps a member of your small group at church would be best or even a Christian peer in the business community. Are you a homemaker? Find a kindred spirit in the neighborhood to meet with over coffee while the kids are asleep or in school. College student? Try meeting with a classmate or a campus representative from a church or parachurch ministry.

Select someone older or younger, but of the same sex. But he or she *must* be someone you can trust. Remember, this person's going to get to know a lot about you.

Set up a meeting and simply present the idea to your friend. You might be surprised how much he or she needs and desires accountability too. Start meeting on a regular basis. And come prepared. You can structure the meeting however you like, but the point is to be direct and honest. If you need some questions to get started, try these:

- Have you spent time daily in prayer and in the Scriptures this week?

- Have you fulfilled the mandate of your calling this week?

- Have you taken time off to be with your family this week?

- Have you been completely above reproach in all your financial dealings this week?

- Have you been with a member of the opposite sex this week in such a way that was inappropriate or could have looked to others as though you were using poor judgment?

- Have you sought out any explicit material this week?

- Have you just lied?[9]

Stay with it, even if it's awkward at first. Evaluate the sessions after five or six meetings. You might want to modify the questions or format.

The important thing, though, is to *do* it.

---

9. Adapted from Swindoll, *The Bride*, pp. 181–82 (page citations are to the second printing).

 *Living Insights*   STUDY TWO

Few things can ruin a marriage quicker than a spouse without integrity. And the union between the bride of Christ and her Groom is no exception. What do people say about your local church's relationship with the Groom? Is she truly committed, or just going through the motions—"playing church"? Is her character as solid and pure as a gold wedding band? Or does it bend under the pressure to attract new members or construct new buildings? Are her eyes fixed on the Groom? Or do competing affections—more elaborate programs, nicer facilities—cause them to wander?

Pretend for a moment that you're not you. Rather, you're a secret observer—someone who's been asked to describe your local church and assess her character. What would this observer report? Write down your findings.

Is your congregation's integrity intact? Do you see any flaws that might cause a scandal if ignored? What steps can you take to communicate or correct them?

Before whipping out your stationery and writing a letter to your pastor, consider first *your own* realm of responsibility. Do you conduct your life and ministry with honesty and authenticity? What can you improve?

Can you serve in or help lead a ministry that needs a shot of integrity? How can you help your pastor maintain his integrity? How about praying for his moral stamina on a regular basis? What else can you do to bolster your church?

Now if you do need to approach someone whose integrity is clearly slipping, write down some things you'd like to tell that person—remembering Paul's words to the Ephesians:

> Speaking the truth in love, we are to grow up in all aspects into Him, who is the head, even Christ, from whom the whole body, being fitted and held together by that which every joint supplies, according to the proper working of each individual part, causes the growth of the body for the building up of itself in love. (Eph. 4:15–16)

_____

_____

Chapter 10

RESTORING RESPECT FOR THE MINISTRY

Selected Scriptures

Your license and registration, sir."

The state trooper was all business. His voice and expression were flat. Flat as his haircut. Flat as the brim of his hat. Flat as the stretch of Kansas highway he monitored. The caravan of two buses and two trucks—each with "Miracles and Wonders" painted on their sides—was doing eighty in a fifty-five. No discussion necessary. Just the license and registration. He flipped open his flat ticket book and started to write.

But Jonas Nightingale knew how to work people. He knew that behind those dark glasses was a heart—a wheel of emotions he could spin and stop at will. He just needed a little time. He attempted some obnoxious humor, but that only annoyed the trooper, who finally handcuffed Nightingale, escorted him to the backseat of the patrol car, and began to read him his rights.

Back in the passenger bus, the other members of the traveling miracle show laid bets on Nightingale's chances of talking his way out of a ticket and jail. Eavesdropping on the conversation via the preacher's hidden microphone, they wondered if the master of manipulation had found a stone soul too heavy to move.

But Nightingale read the signs well. No wedding ring. A Catholic cross dangling from the rear-view mirror. A violin case on the floorboard. He pieced together the officer's past in seconds. His name was Lowell. He had an ex-wife and an estranged daughter, Cathy. He had taught her to play "Claire de Lune" on the violin. He missed her; they hadn't spoken in a year. The preacher wielded words like a chisel on Lowell's emotions, until the stone cop cracked.

Lowell unlocked the cuffs, then called his daughter from Nightingale's bus. He even donated twenty dollars to the itinerant ministry. Lowell went home a blessed man. For Jonas Nightingale, though, it was business as usual. Another heart and wallet had been moved by the miracle of manipulation.

"Thank ya, Jeeesus!" the preacher quipped as the caravan eased back onto the freeway.

Hollywood is rarely kind to the ministry, as demonstrated by Steve Martin's portrayal of Jonas Nightingale in the movie *Leap of Faith*. Yet we can't heap all the blame on Hollywood for such caricatures of Christianity. After all, we provide them with plenty of material.

Realistic Glimpses of the Shameful Scene

There's nothing new about ministers who sin. Even the purest of preachers has flaws. The apostle Paul, while reflecting on the gift of God's grace, called himself the foremost of sinners.

> It is a trustworthy statement, deserving full acceptance,
> that Christ Jesus came into the world to save sinners,
> among whom I am foremost of all. (1 Tim. 1:15)

Violation of God's standards among the clergy, however, has never been more flagrant than now. Ministers make the tabloids and talk shows with embarrassing frequency. News stories reveal a scandalous decay of integrity in a once respected and revered profession. Do you remember these headlines:

Televangelist Confesses Tryst with Prostitute; Resigns in Tears

Hidden Cameras Expose Fraudulent "Healing" Services

Preacher Pleads "Send Money or God Will Take Me Home"

TV Minister Imprisoned for Embezzlement

Those are just a few of the cases that have passed before the probing gaze of the national media. But local, less prominent scandals also scar the church and its reputation, as many more pastors, youth directors, elders, missionaries, counselors, and educators succumb to their passions. You may even have your own story of a Christian leader who violated your trust. Warren Wiersbe laments our predicament:

> Both the ministry and the message of the church
> have lost credibility before a watching world, and
> the world seems to be enjoying the spectacle.[1]

1. Warren W. Wiersbe, *The Integrity Crisis* (Nashville, Tenn.: Thomas Nelson Publishers, Oliver Nelson, 1988), pp. 17–18.

It's time for the bride of Christ to turn heads because of her purity, not her promiscuity. It's time to restore respect for the ministry.

Helpful Facts That Are Easily Forgotten

Restoration must begin with some clear thinking—which means *realistic* thinking. All of the evils we see can easily make us overwhelmed pessimists, so zeroed in on immediate wrongs that we lose any sense of perspective and motivation to stimulate change. The following three facts will help provide a needed balance so that we can take fresh courage in restoring respect for the ministry.

One: *Scripture predicts and warns us of such times.* Though scandals are shameful and shocking, they should not be surprising. The Scriptures tell us over and over that we should expect this in the last days.

> But the Spirit explicitly says that in later times some will fall away from the faith, paying attention to deceitful spirits and doctrines of demons, by means of the hypocrisy of liars seared in their own conscience as with a branding iron. . . .
> In pointing out these things to the brethren, you will be a good servant of Christ Jesus, constantly nourished on the words of the faith and of the sound doctrine which you have been following. (1 Tim. 4:1–2, 6)

People who started out on God's side will change teams. Ministers who once embraced the truth will deliberately distort it to fit their fancy. Paul's ancient warning to Timothy sounds as fresh as today's headlines.

Jesus, too, predicted the rise of false prophets in the end times.

> And Jesus answered and said to them, "See to it that no one misleads you. For many will come in My name, saying, 'I am the Christ,' and will mislead many. . . . And many false prophets will arise, and will mislead many." (Matt. 24:4–5, 11)

So, first of all, don't panic. God's program for the ages is not crumbling. He saw the squall of moral decay blowing in long before it ever got here. In His time, He will subdue it. Meanwhile, His church will survive—for the gates of hell will not overpower it (see Matt. 16:18).

Two: *The actual percentage of those who fall in ministry is quite small.* This is easy to forget because the media don't spotlight above-board ministries. They ignore the thousands of pastors who have a history of faithfully following Christ and feeding His flock. So some of us get a skewed impression. We think, as Elijah did, that "I alone am left" to uphold God's integrity (see 1 Kings 19:14–18). Yes, some leaders will fall. But let's not forget the throngs that refuse to bow the knee to Baal.

Three: *Human imperfection includes ministers.* We've all wandered away from our Shepherd at times—ministers included. When God adopted us into His family, He adopted sinners (see Rom. 3:9–18, 23). That's no excuse for moral misconduct—God still calls Christian leaders to a high and holy standard. But we all need to own up to our tendency toward sin. That's the first step to keeping it in check.

In case you've forgotten that God uses sinners, consider these influential but imperfect saints of old:

> Aaron, Moses' brother, who crafted a golden calf
> for the Israelites to worship
> Samson, who was a notorious womanizer
> David, who committed adultery and arranged a
> murder
> Solomon, who ditched wisdom for self-indulgence
> Isaiah, a "man of unclean lips"
> Gehazi, Elisha's servant, who craved material
> things
> Jonah, who ran from God
> Peter, who denied the Lord in His most difficult
> time
> John Mark, who deserted Paul and Barnabas
> when they needed him the most

If it can happen to them, it can happen to us. The Christian leader who considers himself or herself out of the reach of sin is asking for trouble (see 1 Cor. 10:12).

Unaltered Standard for Those in Ministry

Since we're all tainted with sin, should we lower the standard for ministers? By no means! God expects ministers to model godliness. His qualifications for leadership are clear. Paul outlines them earlier in his first letter to Timothy.

> It is a trustworthy statement: if any man aspires
> to the office of overseer, it is a fine work he desires
> to do. An overseer, then, must be above reproach,
> the husband of one wife, temperate, prudent, re-
> spectable, hospitable, able to teach, not addicted to
> wine or pugnacious, but gentle, uncontentious, free
> from the love of money. He must be one who man-
> ages his own household well, keeping his children
> under control with all dignity (but if a man does not
> know how to manage his own household, how will
> he take care of the church of God?); and not a new
> convert, lest he become conceited and fall into the
> condemnation incurred by the devil. And he must
> have a good reputation with those outside the church,
> so that he may not fall into reproach and the snare
> of the devil. (1 Tim. 3:1–7; see also Titus 1:5–9)

What a job description! Clearly, Christian leadership is not to
be taken lightly. Those considering a career in the clergy or a
position as an elder must carefully evaluate their lives and calling.
In fact, James warns,

> Let not many of you become teachers, my breth-
> ren, knowing that as such we shall incur a stricter
> judgment. (James 3:1)

God entrusts Christian leaders with the spiritual care of His
flock. He wants humble shepherds, not hungry wolves. By taking
His standards seriously, we can reduce the risk of putting unquali-
fied, even dangerous, people in charge.

Ways to Avoid Doubt and Devastation

Because of sin, leaders will continue to fall. However, a fallen
minister need not destroy our faith in the ministry—if we will keep in
mind the things we should refuse, remember, release, and refocus on.[2]

---

2. This section was adapted from the study guide *What It Takes to Win*, coauthored by Bryce
Klabunde, from the Bible-teaching ministry of Charles R. Swindoll (Anaheim, Calif.: Insight
for Living, 1993), pp. 112–14.

Refuse to Deify Anyone in the Ministry

Refuse to put leaders on a pedestal, regardless of their gifts or abilities. We should respect them, appreciate them, acknowledge God's hand in their lives . . . but we should not enthrone them. Instead, as we learn from their example, let's keep in mind that they're as fallible as we are.

And ministers, reject the worship of your parishioners. Follow the example of Paul and Barnabas, who, when the citizens of Lystra tried to worship them as gods, cried out: "We are also men of the same nature as you" (Acts 14:15). You may get a nice view from atop a pedestal, but you'll also make an easy target. It was in Lystra, remember, that Paul's enemies stoned him (v. 19).

Remember that the Flesh Is Weak and the Adversary Is Real

Jesus opened Peter's eyes to the Evil One's lurking presence:

> "Simon, Simon, behold, Satan has demanded permission to sift you like wheat; but I have prayed for you, that your faith may not fail; and you, when once you have turned again, strengthen your brothers." (Luke 22:31–32)

No leader should take Jesus' words lightly. For

> there is not an effective, gifted minister today who is not the target of the Devil and/or his demons. Nor is there a minister strong enough in himself or herself to withstand the adversary's snare. It takes prayer. Prevailing prayer. It also takes being accountable, teachable, and open. Why? Because the enemy is so subtle. You see, no one deliberately makes *plans* to fail in the ministry. No minister ever sat on the side of his bed one morning and said, "Let's see, how can I ruin my reputation today?" But with the weakness of the flesh, mixed with the strength and reality of the adversary, failure is an ever-present possibility. Let him who thinks he stands, I repeat, take heed.[3]

3. Charles R. Swindoll, from the book *The Bride: Renewing Our Passion for the Church* (Grand Rapids, Mich.: Zondervan Publishing House, 1994), p. 203 (page citation is to the second printing).

Release All Judgment to God

There are better ways to keep a leader humble than launching anonymous letters written in rage with a poison pen. Instead, we should encourage our pastors, get to know them personally, and, if necessary, lovingly confront a weakness. But let's leave the judging in the Lord's hands.

Refocus Your Attention on the Ministries That Are Still on Target

This is easier said than done, especially for someone whose spirit is still bleeding from the piercing fall of a once-trusted minister. Words alone can't heal those wounds or erase painful memories. If you've been wounded, the specter of grief may hover over your life for a time, maybe a long time. But try hard to resist the temptation to withdraw into disbelief or bitterness.

Rather, look to Christ. He is still Lord. He is still bigger than that fallible human minister or that slipping ministry. What's gone on is no mystery to Him, and neither is the distress of your heart. He cares deeply when His holy name is vandalized—not because He is vain—but because He doesn't want us to stumble on the way to our only sure Refuge. Don't take our word for it; take God's in Ezekiel 34:1–16, where He promises to comfort His sheep who have been abused by sinful shepherds.

And look to other ministries or even denominations that are still honoring Him. You may be surprised at the places where you'll find His healing touch. And you may be delighted to discover that you *can* give again, you *can* trust again, you *can* serve the Lord with joy again.[4]

Living Insights STUDY ONE

Only one headline could ruin Christianity:

Bones of Jesus Christ Found

If archaeologists proved beyond a shadow of a doubt that they had unearthed the remains of our Lord, Christianity would crumble.

4. If you've been hurt by a fallen pastor or Christian leader and need some encouragement to keep going, we recommend Ted Kitchen's book *Aftershock: What to Do When Leaders and Others Fail You* (Portland, Oreg.: Multnomah Press, 1992).

Our system of belief hinges on the resurrection of Christ. If He's still in the grave, then He didn't rise as He said He would. Which would mean He's not who He said He was. So death beat Him, and there is no one to save us from our sin. No wonder Paul, when he wanted to convince the Corinthians of the centrality of the resurrection, said to them, "If Christ has not been raised, your faith is worthless; you are still in your sins" (1 Cor. 15:17).

Don't worry. The bones of our risen Savior will never turn up. His tomb is forever empty, because He sits at the right hand of God the Father. Our faith is secure.

But headlines about fallen ministers may have discouraged you, causing you to question the validity of Christianity. If so, that's understandable. But remember that the foundation of our faith is Christ Himself, not sinful humans. Jesus is real. Jesus is risen. And Jesus will be around long after the newspapers turn yellow. So don't look in the paper for perfection. Look in the Bible. That's where you'll find His story.

No headline will ever nullify the Christian faith, but one will certainly generate some discussion:

Jesus Christ Returns for His Bride

See you at the wedding feast!

 Living Insights STUDY TWO

Thanks for joining us in this study of the bride of Christ. We've been gazing at ourselves in the mirror for ten chapters now. What do you see in the reflection? A clearer purpose for the church? The beauty of a unique style? Character that needs touching up? And what about the Groom—are you anxious to see Him? What would you change before He returns?

Take a moment to write down any key thoughts that stand out from each chapter. They may apply to you as an individual or to your local church. Record them in any form you like—an action to take, a principle to remember, even a praise to lift up to God.

Our Purpose _____

_____

Our Objectives _____

86

A Genuine Concern for Others_____

A Contagious Style_____

The Difference between a Metropolitan and a Neighborhood Men-
tality_____

What Changes and What Doesn't_____

Ministering in the Last Days _____

"Stayin' Ready 'til Quittin' Time" _____

The Value of Integrity _____

Restoring Respect for the Ministry _____

BOOKS FOR PROBING FURTHER

Though we've taken a long, thoughtful look at the bride in this study, we've only begun to get to know her. If you want to learn more about her character, her priorities, even her relationship with the Groom, use the following bibliography to extend your study of the church. That way, you can continue the wedding celebration for as long as you like!

Bennis, Warren, and Burt Nanus. *Leaders: The Strategies for Taking Charge*. New York, N.Y.: Harper and Row, Publishers, 1985.

Bridges, Jerry. *The Pursuit of Holiness*. Colorado Springs, Colo.: NavPress, 1978.

Coleman, Robert E. *The Master Plan of Evangelism*. 2d edition. Old Tappan, N.J.: Fleming H. Revell Co., Power Books, 1964.

Colson, Charles, with Ellen Santilli Vaughn. *The Body*. Dallas, Tex.: Word Publishing, 1992.

Getz, Gene A. *A Biblical Theology of Material Possessions*. Chicago, Ill.: Moody Press, 1990.

———. *Serving One Another*. Wheaton, Ill.: Scripture Press Publications, Victor Books, 1984.

———. *Sharpening the Focus of the Church*. Revised edition. Wheaton, Ill.: Scripture Press Publications, Victor Books, 1984.

Hendricks, Howard G. *Teaching to Change Lives*. Portland, Oreg.: Multnomah Press; Walk Thru the Bible Ministries, 1987.

Ortlund, Anne. *Up with Worship: How to Quit Playing Church*. Revised edition. Ventura, Calif.: Regal Books, 1982.

Petersen, Jim. *Living Proof*. Colorado Springs, Colo.: NavPress, 1989.

Peterson, Eugene. *Under the Unpredictable Plant: An Exploration in Vocational Holiness*. Grand Rapids, Mich.: William B. Eerdmans Publishing Co., 1992.

———. *Working the Angles: The Shape of Pastoral Integrity*. Grand

Rapids, Mich.: William B. Eerdmans Publishing Co., 1987.

Smith, Fred. *Learning to Lead: Bringing Out the Best in People*. Carol Stream, Ill.: Christianity Today; Dallas, Tex.: Word Books, Publisher, 1986.

Snyder, Howard A. *The Problem of Wine Skins*. Downers Grove, Ill.: InterVarsity Press, 1975.

Stedman, Ray C. *Body Life*. 3d edition. Ventura, Calif.: Regal Books, 1979.

Stott, John R. W. *Guard the Gospel: The Message of 2 Timothy*. The Bible Speaks Today series. Downers Grove, Ill.: InterVarsity Press, 1973.

————. *The Spirit, the Church, and the World: The Message of Acts*. Downers Grove, Ill.: InterVarsity Press, 1990.

Swindoll, Charles R. *The Bride: Renewing Our Passion for the Church*. Grand Rapids, Mich.: Zondervan Publishing House, 1994.

Thompson, Robert R., and Gerald R. Thompson. *Organizing for Accountability: How to Avoid Crisis in Your Nonprofit Ministry*. Wheaton, Ill.: Harold Shaw Publishers, 1991.

Tozer, A. W. *The Pursuit of God*. Camp Hill, Pa.: Christian Publications, 1982.

Wiersbe, Warren W. *The Integrity Crisis*. Nashville, Tenn.: Thomas Nelson Publishers, Oliver Nelson, 1988.

Wiersbe, Warren W., and David Wiersbe. *Making Sense of the Ministry*. Grand Rapids, Mich.: Baker Book House, 1989.

Some of these books may be out of print and available only through a library. For those currently available, please contact your local Christian bookstore. Books by Charles R. Swindoll may be obtained through Insight for Living. IFL also offers some books by other authors—please note the ordering information that follows and contact the office that serves you.

ORDERING INFORMATION

THE BRIDE
Cassette Tapes and Study Guide

This Bible study guide was designed to be used independently or in conjunction with the broadcast of Chuck Swindoll's taped messages which are listed below. If you would like to order cassette tapes or further copies of this study guide, please see the information given below and the order form provided at the end of this guide.

		U.S.	Canada
BRD	Study guide	$ 3.95 ea.	$ 5.25 ea.
BRDCS	Cassette series, includes all individual tapes, album cover, and one complimentary study guide	36.25	44.75 ea.
BRD 1–5	Individual cassettes, includes messages A and B	6.30 ea.	8.00 ea.

The prices are subject to change without notice.

BRD 1-A: *Our Purpose*—Selected Scriptures
     B: *Our Objectives*—Acts 2:41–47

BRD 2-A: *A Genuine Concern for Others*—Acts 2:41–47; 3:1–8
     B: *A Contagious Style*—1 Thessalonians 2:1–13

BRD 3-A: *The Difference between a Metropolitan and a Neighborhood Mentality*—Exodus 18:7–24; Ephesians 4:11–16
     B: *What Changes and What Doesn't*—Selected Scriptures

BRD 4-A: *Ministering in the Last Days*—2 Timothy 3; Matthew 24:3–12
     B: *"Stayin' Ready 'til Quittin' Time"*—2 Timothy 3:10–4:8

BRD 5-A: *The Value of Integrity**—Selected Scriptures
     B: *Restoring Respect for the Ministry**—Selected Scriptures

* These messages were not a part of the original series be are compatible with it.

How to Order by Phone or FAX
(Credit card orders only)

United States: 1-800-772-8888 from 7:00 A.M. to 4:30 P.M., Pacific time, Monday through Friday
FAX (714) 575-5496 anytime, day or night

Canada: 1-800-663-7639, Vancouver residents call (604) 596-2910 from 7:00 A.M. to 5:00 P.M., Pacific time, Monday through Friday
FAX (604) 596-2975 anytime, day or night

Australia: (03) 872-4606 or FAX (03) 874-8890 from 8:00 A.M. to 5:00 P.M., Monday through Friday

Other International Locations: call the Ordering Services Department in the United States at (714) 575-5000 during the hours listed above.

How to Order by Mail

United States
- Mail to: Ordering Services Department
  Insight for Living
  Post Office Box 69000
  Anaheim, CA 92817-0900
- Sales tax: California residents add 7.25%.
- Shipping: add 10% of the total order amount for first-class delivery. (Otherwise, allow four to six weeks for fourth-class delivery.)
- Payment: personal checks, money orders, credit cards (Visa, Master-Card, Discover Card, and American Express). No invoices or COD orders available.
- $10 fee for *any* returned check.

Canada
- Mail to: Insight for Living Ministries
  Post Office Box 2510
  Vancouver, BC V6B 3W7
- Sales tax: please add 7% GST. British Columbia residents also add 7% sales tax (on tapes or cassette series).
- Shipping: included in prices listed above.
- Payment: personal checks, money orders, credit cards (Visa, Master-Card). No invoices or COD orders available.
- Delivery: approximately four weeks.

Australia and the South Pacific
- Mail to: Insight for Living, Inc.
  GPO Box 2823 EE
  Melbourne, Victoria 3001, Australia
- Shipping: add 25% to the total order.
- Delivery: approximately four to six weeks.
- Payment: personal checks payable in Australian funds, international money orders, or credit cards (Visa, MasterCard, and BankCard).

Other International Locations
- Mail to: Ordering Services Department
  Insight for Living
  Post Office Box 69000
  Anaheim, CA 92817-0900
- Shipping and delivery time: please see chart that follows.
- Payment: personal checks payable in U.S. funds, international money orders, or credit cards (Visa, MasterCard, and American Express).

Type of Shipping	Postage Cost	Delivery
Surface	10% of total order*	6 to 10 weeks
Airmail	25% of total order*	under 6 weeks

*Use U.S. price as a base.

Our Guarantee

Your complete satisfaction is our top priority here at Insight for Living. If you're not completely satisfied with anything you order, please return it for full credit, a refund, or a replacement, as you prefer.

Insight for Living Catalog

The Insight for Living catalog features study guides, tapes, and books by a variety of Christian authors. To obtain a free copy, call us at the numbers listed above.

Order Form
United States, Australia, and Other International Locations
(Canadian residents please use order form on reverse side.)

BRDCS represents the entire *The Bride* series in a special album cover, while BRD 1–5 are the individual tapes included in the series. BRD represents this study guide, should you desire to order additional copies.

BRD	Study guide	$ 3.95 ea.
BRDCS	Cassette series,	36.25
	includes all individual tapes, album cover, and one complimentary study guide	
BRD 1–5	Individual cassettes,	6.30 ea.
	includes messages A and B	

Product Code	Product Description	Quantity	Unit Price	Total
			$	$
		Subtotal		
California Residents—Sales Tax *Add 7.25% of subtotal.*				
U.S. First-Class Shipping *For faster delivery, add 10% for postage and handling.*				
Non-United States Residents *Australia add 25% for shipping and handling.* *All other locations: U.S. price plus 10% surface postage or 25% airmail.*				
Gift to Insight for Living *Tax-deductible in the United States.*				
Total Amount Due *Please do not send cash.*				$

Prices are subject to change without notice.

Payment by: ❑ Check or money order payable to Insight for Living ❑ Credit card

(Circle one): Visa MasterCard Discover Card American Express BankCard (In Australia)

Number _____

Expiration Date _____ Signature _____
We cannot process your credit card purchase without your signature.

Name _____

Address _____

City _____ State _____

Zip Code _____ Country _____

Telephone (____) _____ Radio Station ____ ____ ____ ____
If questions arise concerning your order, we may need to contact you.

Mail this order form to the Ordering Services Department at one of these addresses:

Insight for Living
Post Office Box 69000, Anaheim, CA 92817-0900

Insight for Living, Inc.
GPO Box 2823 EE, Melbourne, VIC 3001, Australia

Order Form
Canadian Residents

(Residents of the United States, Australia, and other international locations,
please use order form on reverse side.)

BRDCS represents the entire *The Bride* series in a special album cover, while BRD 1–5 are the individual tapes included in the series. BRD represents this study guide, should you desire to order additional copies.

BRD	Study guide	$ 5.25 ea.
BRDCS	Cassette series,	44.75
	includes all individual tapes, album cover,	
	and one complimentary study guide	
BRD 1–5	Individual cassettes,	8.00 ea.
	includes messages A and B	

Product Code	Product Description	Quantity	Unit Price	Total
			$	$
		Subtotal		
		Add 7% GST		
	British Columbia Residents *Add 7% sales tax on individual tapes or cassette series.*			
	Gift to Insight for Living Ministries *Tax-deductible in Canada.*			
	Total Amount Due *Please do not send cash.*		$	

Prices are subject to change without notice.

Payment by: ❑ Check or money order payable to Insight for Living Ministries
❑ Credit card

(Circle one): Visa   MasterCard   Number _____

Expiration Date _____ Signature _____
We cannot process your credit card purchase without your signature.

Name _____

Address _____

City _____ Province _____

Postal Code _____ Country _____

Telephone (___) _____ Radio Station ____ ____ ____ ____
If questions arise concerning your order, we may need to contact you.

Mail this order form to the Ordering Services Department at the following address:

Insight for Living Ministries
Post Office Box 2510
Vancouver, BC, Canada V6B 3W7

Order Form
United States, Australia, and Other International Locations
(Canadian residents please use order form on reverse side.)

BRDCS represents the entire *The Bride* series in a special album cover, while BRD 1–5 are the individual tapes included in the series. BRD represents this study guide, should you desire to order additional copies.

BRD	Study guide	$ 3.95 ea.
BRDCS	Cassette series,	36.25
	includes all individual tapes, album cover,	
	and one complimentary study guide	
BRD 1–5	Individual cassettes,	6.30 ea.
	includes messages A and B	

Product Code	Product Description	Quantity	Unit Price	Total
			$	$
		Subtotal		
	California Residents—Sales Tax *Add 7.25% of subtotal.*			
	U.S. First-Class Shipping *For faster delivery, add 10% for postage and handling.*			
	Non-United States Residents *Australia add 25% for shipping and handling.* *All other locations: U.S. price plus 10% surface postage or 25% airmail.*			
	Gift to Insight for Living *Tax-deductible in the United States.*			
	Total Amount Due *Please do not send cash.*		$	

Prices are subject to change without notice.

Payment by: ❏ Check or money order payable to Insight for Living ❏ Credit card

(Circle one): Visa   MasterCard   Discover Card   American Express   BankCard (In Australia)

Number _____

Expiration Date _____ Signature _____
We cannot process your credit card purchase without your signature.

Name _____

Address _____

City _____ State _____

Zip Code _____ Country _____

Telephone ( ) _____ Radio Station ____ ____ ____ ____
If questions arise concerning your order, we may need to contact you.

Mail this order form to the Ordering Services Department at one of these addresses:

Insight for Living
Post Office Box 69000, Anaheim, CA 92817-0900

Insight for Living, Inc.
GPO Box 2823 EE, Melbourne, VIC 3001, Australia

Order Form
Canadian Residents
(Residents of the United States, Australia, and other international locations, please use order form on reverse side.)

BRDCS represents the entire *The Bride* series in a special album cover, while BRD 1–5 are the individual tapes included in the series. BRD represents this study guide, should you desire to order additional copies.

BRD	Study guide	$ 5.25 ea.
BRDCS	Cassette series, includes all individual tapes, album cover, and one complimentary study guide	44.75
BRD 1–5	Individual cassettes, includes messages A and B	8.00 ea.

Product Code	Product Description	Quantity	Unit Price	Total
			$	$
		Subtotal		
		Add 7% GST		
		British Columbia Residents *Add 7% sales tax on individual tapes or cassette series.*		
		Gift to Insight for Living Ministries *Tax-deductible in Canada.*		
		Total Amount Due *Please do not send cash.*	$	

Prices are subject to change without notice.

Payment by: ❏ Check or money order payable to Insight for Living Ministries
❏ Credit card

(Circle one): Visa   MasterCard   Number _____

Expiration Date _____   Signature _____
We cannot process your credit card purchase without your signature.

Name _____

Address _____

City _____ Province _____

Postal Code _____ Country _____

Telephone (_____) _____ Radio Station ____ ____ ____ ____
If questions arise concerning your order, we may need to contact you.

Mail this order form to the Ordering Services Department at the following address:

Insight for Living Ministries
Post Office Box 2510
Vancouver, BC, Canada V6B 3W7